# Municipal Knowledge Series

# PLACES and SPACES

# GORD HUME

*brought to you by the publishers of*

## Municipal World
### CANADA'S MUNICIF

Library and Archives Canada Cataloguing in Publication

Hume, Gord, author
    Places and spaces / Gord Hume.

(Municipal knowledge series)
ISBN 978-1-926843-12-4 (pbk.)

     1. City planning.  2. Public spaces.  3. Cities and towns.
I. Title.  II. Series: Municipal knowledge series

HT166.H86 2014      307.1'216      C2014-904764-9

Published in Canada by
Municipal World Inc.
42860 Sparta Line
Union, Ontario N0L 2L0
mwadmin@municipalworld.com
www.municipalworld.com

ITEM 0038
Municipal World – Reg. T.M. in Canada Municipal World Inc.

The text pages of this book are printed on:

# TABLE OF CONTENTS

# FOREWORD

*"We will neglect our cities to our peril, for in neglecting them we neglect the nation." – John F. Kennedy*

Cities and towns are living entities. People make them pulse with energy and excitement. We share experiences; we learn and grow; we walk alone, and then we celebrate with thousands. We fall in love, start families, build careers, and grow old. Childhood experiences – sights, smells, and sounds – help to form us as adults, and those memories can be awakened many years later upon returning. We seldom lose our love for our "home town."

We instinctively understand place as being important – family, safety, fun, growing, exploring. Home.

Great public places and spaces help to create vibrant communities and local prosperity, and they can provide a wonderful quality of life for residents and visitors.

It is this exploration of the public realm that forms the nucleus of this book – how municipalities use, abuse, and celebrate their unique opportunity to shape and re-shape the design, development, and future of their towns and cities. It is about people and how they connect and live.

The unique intersection of form, function, and beauty – how places and spaces set a tone and style for a community and how people use and respond to them – configures every city in the world.

Some do it successfully. Many less so. Some are changing as they recognize the importance of their municipal environment. Some cities are realizing they are not sustainable continuing on the path they have followed for decades. Growing social and environmental problems are forcing change in communities. Brutal economic reality is being thrust upon others, with municipal leaders jarred by cities declaring bankruptcy.

Cities and their future are at a unique moment in time. We are discovering new and often better ways to design and operate our communities. As the world becomes ever-more urban, the path chosen for our communities will shape the future of our global society.

We need greater clarity in understanding this connectivity between people and their cities. We need a generation of leaders who will link the physical realm to the social, cultural, environmental, and economic health and prosperity of their communities.

How municipalities shape and design the public realm strongly influences their image and style. A heritage of wonderful architecture and built form (along with a history of demanding great public spaces) tells the story of cities that have lasted millennia. We are warmed by this, inspired by the shape and feel of the physical presence of magnificent places, and delighted by the social interaction of appealing public spaces.

People have an almost instinctual desire for beauty and peace in their surroundings. Aesthetics matter to us. We like trees and green spaces; we adore water and waterfronts.

Places and spaces help to shape the civility of cities and the people in them. We are inspired by the physical presence of unique and lasting design. Magnificent architecture can define a city – think of Antoni Gaudi's influence on Barcelona. He set a style and vibe for design and public art that weaves its way throughout the city, and today inspires Barcelona as a beacon for creative industries and minds.

Places and spaces define a city: Soaring towers that pierce the sky. Verdant, lush parks where children play and laugh. Gorgeous bridges that curve elegantly over a river or harbour. The energy that comes with glowing, colourful light displays in a bustling social district where music drifts over diners on a sidewalk patio. The respect for a well-preserved heritage property that adds an elegant tone to a neighbourhood. What a drab, sour life we would have if wonderful architecture and design didn't bring to life the places around us. How sad it would be if we couldn't enjoy the rhythm and passion of life on our streets and sidewalks.

How the public and private realms intersect – and sometime collide – can be a defining moment for a community.

How different would our history and culture be if people hadn't gathered over the centuries and used public spaces for celebration – and revolution?

Every community is absolutely distinctive and unique. But, a common thread is that municipal councils have substantial control of the physical realm and can generally determine what happens to that space.

I remember, as a rookie city councillor in the 1990s, receiving my first big subdivision application. What I particularly remember was an overwhelming sense of disappointment: it just seemed to be the same-old, same-old.

As the process proceeded, I began to feel as if I was abruptly thrust into a three-dimensional chess game where there was no winner. Nobody was on same plane. Developers seemed more focused on their profit projections than designing and building a wonderful new community. The neighbourhood delivered some shrill comments and divided opinions, but people were generally ineffective in communicating their concerns or alternatives. Planners and engineers focused more on their rule books than on interesting design, and seemed quite uninterested in innovative ideas. Council members were bouncing all over the board. Public engagement was desultory at best.

Everybody was talking, but nobody was communicating. Surely we can do better.

For far too long, this combative relationship has hurt urban design and subverted exciting new concepts. Too often, this stark divide permeates council discussions. Development issues are rarely clear-cut. We need to encourage innovation and creativity that meets both community and business needs; unfortunately, that happens infrequently.

Communities that want to move ahead must push through this quagmire and insist on bold thinking and productive partnerships. Municipalities must become smart enough to support interesting design and creative ideas that meet the public good, and still allow developers to make a reasonable return on their investment.

Like many people, I watched in dismay through the 70s and 80s as downtowns deteriorated or were hollowed out; people left and stores closed as the great suburban/mall era flourished with a vengeance. Heritage buildings were left to rot or were torn down indiscriminately.

By the 90s, cities were often facing dramatic urban crises, frequently of their own making. Other orders of government, never very invested in working with or supporting municipalities, had abandoned public housing and most public transportation planning, leaving municipalities very much on their own.

Do municipalities need a crisis to act? Do municipalities really anticipate supportive, positive actions from the legislature or parliament? Our cities and towns need to break away from "big brother" and get the authority and fiscal opportunities necessary to compete in the global economy – an environment increasingly being dominated by strong cities and metropolitan regions.

Attracting, retaining, and developing talent is a core function for prosperous cities. Building and reshaping sustainable, dynamic communities is a crucial role for local governments. Much economic growth in the 21st century is being driven by city-to-city networks and relationships.

The connection is now quite clear between planning and prosperity. It is also very clear that planning and public health are closely aligned. Vibrant urban design and sustainable development are critical for prosperous, healthy, and successful communities.

As an elected official, it takes time to learn the system and the vocabulary that goes with planning and development. The industry – from councillors to bureaucrats, from designers to developers – has not always attracted people interested in bold, creative design and really exciting, different ways of doing business and building great public places and spaces.

Sadly, it is often city hall that is the greatest impediment.

******

To stretch a golf analogy, there aren't many mulligans in planning, and we've been out of bounds too often. The planning decisions we make today will shape a community for the next 50 to 100 years. That is one of the biggest reasons that we need to do better.

We don't have to bulldoze every tree and mound in sight. Everybody supports in-fill projects – until it is in their backyard. NIMBYism lives. Snout-houses (those with big two- or three-car garages pointed prominently to the street) don't promote close neighbourhood interaction. Subdivisions built without sidewalks are just a really bad idea.

If we're going to push residents into living in the suburbs, far from where they work, why are we suddenly surprised by the traffic and commuting problems that result?

Badly planned and designed concrete-tower housing projects have ended up as urban ghettoes, with severe social and crime problems that offer little hope to residents. I remember seeing acres of grey, crumbling apartments in the old Soviet Union; there was an overwhelming bleakness to the buildings and the people who lived in them. Dreadful.

Council members often don't know what questions to ask, or what alternatives there might be as they search for clarity and inspiration. The great car explosion decades ago saw thriving neighbourhoods – like St. Roch in Quebec City – cleaved by a new freeway, resulting in 40 years of despair and $400M spent trying to knit it back together. Too often, cities just did bad planning.

There has to be a better way – with a more effective outcome.

Jennifer Keesmaat, the chief city planner for the City of Toronto, observes succinctly and honestly: "Our challenge is that, because we lost our way and our focus as to what we were trying to achieve as a profession, we lost credibility. You often see planners getting beaten up by city councils that don't use data and evidence, and don't use a placemaking model or a model that's rooted in ensuring we're planning for the public interest in a very comprehensive way. We see that take precedent over good planning. As planners, we need to own that problem."

Cities and towns need to change the conversation. We need to rethink urban life. Reviving downtowns. Taking a fresh look at suburban issues like design, transportation, local food accessibility, and sustainability. Confronting the affordability of housing, especially for young people graduating and starting their careers, is a growing problem, particularly in metro regions.

## "The Sidewalk Ballet"

We need to appreciate better what Jane Jacobs referred to so beautifully as "the sidewalk ballet of a lively street." We must place our focus on the people of our communities, and what they want from their streets and neighbourhoods.

Cities need to better recognize and support the importance and value of public places and spaces. We need a greater commitment by urban planners, elected officials, the private sector, and community leaders to build better cities. Local governments must do a better job of planning, protecting, supporting, and animating the public realm.

We need to improve, and we're beginning to do that. That is part of what this book is about – there is hope emerging from thoughtful civic and community leaders who are stepping forward with ideas and passion.

In today's urban society, as housing units get smaller, public spaces and places are becoming the "living rooms" of our society. Not enough elected officials or even professional planners have really grasped this emerging shift and the implications it has for municipalities. Increasingly, these places and spaces will be where people meet, socialize, work, communicate, share, eat, walk, and play.

Planning, zoning, official plans, and the other aspects of growing and building communities are among the relatively few governance aspects for which municipalities have almost complete control. There may be provincial policy statements or parameters, or appeals to the courts or bodies like the Ontario Municipal Board; but, generally, local governments have substantial authority and accountability for planning and zoning decisions.

Shaping a community leaves an enormous legacy for the municipal council and administration of the day. Some would argue these are the most important decisions a council will make during its term, because those decisions will have a far-reaching impact on the economic development of a community, the cultural and social progress of its people, the environmental and sustainability issues that are of growing urgency and importance, and the quality of life the city offers to its residents.

******

As always, my books about municipalities are written from the practical rather than academic point of view. I am neither an architect nor a professional planner. This is my fifth book on local government and building wonderful communities; like those before it, this one comes from the heart, the street, and the council chambers. I hope it provides ideas and guidance and will provoke larger discussions amongst politicians, city hall administration, the development industry, and the community.

This book, also like my others, is written with the passionate belief that, for most people, and most businesses, most of the time, local government is becoming the most important order of government.

Our towns and cities are our homes, so how we make them more civil, enjoyable, and livable is a goal worthy of pursuit. It is crucial for local councils and city halls to meet that challenge and opportunity. The shocking corruption and incompetence that has plagued some city governments (and has emerged into the sunlight of public disgust) proves we still have a long way to go.

Building great cities that can compete in the global hunt for talent and investment is one big step. Canadian and American cities have frequently failed to understand the vast growth and development going on in emerging urban centres in Asia, Africa, Southeast Asia, South America, and other regions. Complacency is no answer.

This book is not about assessing blame – there's lots of that to go around and it serves little purpose. We need the honesty to acknowledge mistakes and problems, and then search for new paths forward. We need to do better, and we can.

Not all communities are the same; a great solution in one city doesn't necessarily translate to another. That is why *local* planning decisions offer distinctive opportunities for ideas and conversations. It is one of the treasures of the civic planning process.

If municipalities continue to focus on developing great communities that are sustainable, prosperous, creative, fun, and exciting, then their legacy can be great.

To help on this journey for *Places and Spaces,* I visited and met with municipal leaders in cities in Australia, New Zealand, and North America, supplemented by my visits over the years to cities in Asia, Europe, and other countries. I am indebted to the many leaders and experts who stepped forward and graciously offered much time, professionalism, and their individual prowess to help shape this book. Their wisdom, experience, insight, and sharing of knowledge and ideas elevates my simple prose, and I thank them profoundly.

In alphabetical order:

***Larry Beasley, C.M.*** – The retired director of planning for the City of Vancouver. He is now the "Distinguished Practice Professor of Planning" at the University of British Columbia and the founding principal of Beasley and Associates, an international planning consultancy. During his 30 years of civic service, Larry Beasley achieved land use and transportation plans that dramatically re-shaped Vancouver's inner city. He is the chief advisor on urban design for the City of Dallas, Texas; a member of the International Economic Development Advisory Board of Rotterdam; and is the special advisor on city planning to the government of Abu Dhabi in the United Arab Emirates. Larry Beasley is a member of the Order of Canada.

**Ludo Campbell-Reid** – The manager of environmental strategy and policy department in Auckland, New Zealand. He is also the design champion for the city. Auckland is going through an amazing trans-formation as it aspires to become one of the world's leading cities. In 2012, the City Centre Master Plan set out a 30-year strategy for Auckland to become an international destination and economic powerhouse. Dramatic use of design and adapting public spaces is an essential part of the city's strategy. Ludo Campbell-Reid leads over 100 planners and designers responsible for boldly reshaping this city of 1.5 million residents.

**Jack Diamond** – Born in South Africa, and now one of Canada's best known architects, with a global reputation. His firm, Diamond Schmitt Architects, has done such major projects around the world as the New Mariinsky Theatre for opera and ballet in St. Petersburg, Russia; the Jerusalem City Hall in Israel; the Harman Center for the Arts in Washington, DC; the Li Ka Shing Knowledge Institute and the Four Seasons Centre for the Performing Arts in Toronto; and many more. He has dealt with all orders of governments, and understands local cultural and social sensitivities. He brings an international perspective to why municipal investment in our public spaces and places is so important.

**Robert Doyle** – The Lord Mayor of Melbourne, Australia. Robert Doyle leads this vibrant and dynamic international city for a second term. He was a member of Victoria's parliament for 14 years and a former leader of the opposition. He was recently appointed to the United Nations Advisory Committee of Local Authorities. As a previous host of the Olympic Games and other major international events, including the prestigious Australian Open tennis tournament, Melbourne is recognized as the most livable city in the world, and a creative powerhouse.

*Jeff Fielding* – A former city planner for Winnipeg and Calgary; CAO for Kitchener and London; city manager for Burlington; and now city manager for Calgary. Jeff Fielding is a graduate of the University of Waterloo, where he obtained both his undergraduate and graduate degrees in urban geography and urban planning. He began his work in municipal government in 1978. He brings great insight into the municipal planning process and the internal issues of city halls.

*Eddie Friel, OBE* – Expert-in-residence at Niagara University's Hospitality and Research Center in New York. With more than 40 years of experience in the public and private sectors of tourism, the arts, and destination marketing, Eddie Friel brings vast experience and success in helping many cities. Of particular note was his role in the regeneration of post-industrial cities (such as Glasgow, Scotland, where he led the bid for the city's designation as a Cultural Capital of Europe). He was awarded the Order of the British Empire. He now consults with cities throughout Europe and North America.

*Jennifer Keesmaat* – Chief city planner for the City of Toronto. Jennifer Keesmaat is a former urban design consultant in the private sector who did master plans and major urban design projects with municipalities across Canada, as well as in the United States, Ireland, and Greece. With both public and private sector experience and expertise, she brings very progressive thinking and ideas to the larger planning challenges facing urban areas. Her insights as a leading municipal planner provide a platform for new ideas about urban planning and design.

*John Nicholson* – Principal for Nicholson Sheffield Architects Inc. The company has done a wide variety of public and private sector work, dealing with many municipalities both large and small. The perspective of a working architect who deals with bureaucrats and local zoning and design regulations was an important addition for this book. His projects have included municipal, library, health care, education, housing, recreational, mixed use, and office buildings. His commitment to the interface between urban design and architecture has resulted in award-winning projects.

**Brian Ohl** – Regional vice president for Global Spectrum in Philadelphia. Brian Ohl has been the general manager of Budweiser Gardens (formerly the John Labatt Centre), since it opened in 2002 in London, Ontario. The nearly 10,000-seat sports and entertainment complex has been credited as one of the new anchors that revitalized London's downtown. As more and more communities consider building such facilities as urban renewal projects, his candid comments about the design and operation are valuable.

**Tessa Virtue** – Together with partner Scott Moir, brought home the gold medal in ice dance at the Vancouver 2010 Olympic Games, and two silver medals from the Sochi 2014 Olympics. They are the most decorated Olympic figure skaters in Canadian history, having also won two World Championships. I interviewed Tessa Virtue at her training complex in Michigan before Sochi. I was intrigued by the perspective of a world-class elite athlete who has performed around the globe, and the impact of local venues, culture, and cities. Her charming candour offers a unique vantage point about why investments in cultural and sports/recreational facilities are vital for municipalities.

******

We have reached a critical moment in time for communities in North America. Several cities in the United States have declared bankruptcy. The largest and most visible was "The Motor City" – caused in part by Detroit's sorry history of municipal corruption, a population that fled the inner city, an inability to renew the local economy in the face of global manufacturing transformation, and an $18.5B debt.

Cities in Canada are struggling with a municipal infrastructure deficit that is growing daily and, by some estimates, is approaching the $1 trillion mark. At the same time, building new cities and renewing old ones around the world is estimated to be a $50+ trillion investment. Urban growth and redevelopment is at a new peak.

If they are going to compete successfully in the global economy, then cities must better understand their physical assets, the management of those resources, the opportunities to develop public places and spaces, and why investments in these critical assets are so vital.

That means new thinking inside city halls, reassessment of traditional procedures, smarter investments in public places and spaces,
and a commitment to building sustainable, livable, and creative
communities offering that great quality of life. It means understanding significant changes in demographics, social structures, and gen-
erational demands.

There will be winners and losers. The battle has begun.

July 2014
<gord@gordhume.com>

*On the cover:* *Melbourne, Australia is the most livable city in the world,
using its waterfront, innovative urban design, treed central core, and the
world's longest tram system to support a walkable, vibrant community.
(Photo: Gord Hume)*

# CHAPTER 1

# IT'S ALL ABOUT THE LAND

*"When you look at a city, it's like reading the hopes, aspirations and pride of everyone who built it." – Hugh Newell Jacobsen*

It starts with the land. As the second-largest nation on earth, Canada has nearly 10 million square kilometres of land. That's almost seven percent of the earth's total.

It's also about the water. We have the third-largest supply of fresh water, behind only Brazil and Russia. In fact, Canada has nearly 20 percent of the world's fresh water, but less than half of that total is renewable. We are the second-most profligate user of water, behind only the U.S.

And, it is about the sky and the air. From when the sun first peeks across the Atlantic Ocean onto the fishing villages of Newfoundland, to the glorious sunsets in Saskatchewan, to the stunning beauty of the Northern Lights in the Northwest Territories, Canada is richly blessed.

And yet ... Canadians are the largest producers of garbage amongst developed countries. Our landfills and garbage dumps are strewn across the nation. We have communities that still use our lakes, rivers, and harbours as their toilet bowl – dumping raw, untreated human sewage into once pristine waters. Our skies are often filled with smog and pollution, choking people and forcing the vulnerable indoors.

Is this the best we can do? Or, is it just a shameful chapter in mankind's long development?

Of the earth's surface (all figures approximate), about 70 percent is water. Of the 30 percent that is land, the majority is uninhabitable – deserts, mountains, arctic landscapes. The United Nations says about 30 percent of the land surface is used for livestock production. Woodlands and forests take about 32 percent, and deserts comprise about 14 percent, according to other studies. Rainforests once covered about 14 percent of the earth's surface; today, scientists estimate it is about six percent.

Cities (where, by 2030, 60 percent of all the people on the planet will live) use up about one percent of the land. Just one percent.

Yet, despite that relatively small footprint, humans consume vast resources. Sustainability is a question that has yet to be answered definitively, but common sense would indicate we need to get smarter and take better care to ensure our planet's future. As we hurtle towards eight billion, then nine billion people living on earth, how we're going to feed people and find fresh, potable water for all is a growing concern.

What human habits, demands, desires, and creations will next be transformed into implements of destruction?

Scientists have produced the first map that traces human influence on the natural world, and the numbers are big, according to *National Geographic*. Overall, 83 percent of the total land surface and 98 percent of the areas where it is possible to grow the world's three main crops (rice, wheat, and maize) are directly influenced by human activities.

This is another reason why local council decisions are so critical. Some scientists argue that land use and development, community sustainability, and feeding our growing population will become the most critical issues of the 21st century. Local politicians tend to be way behind on understanding the importance of this. When you pave over good agricultural land for another suburban development, it has a significant ripple effect on the ecosystem, the ability to support local food production, and our environmental sustainability.

Cities and towns are going to be confronted with some very harsh realities in the decades ahead. Most of them haven't sufficiently considered the future. This is one of the risks of politically-inept elected officials who focus on short-term issues to get re-elected, instead of long-term planning for the benefit of their communities. And, unfortunately, the potential overlap of responsibilities and political obligations often provides an escape for some elected people, who point fingers at other orders of government and say, "It's their responsibility." Accountability can't be blurred.

## Using Natural Resources

There is a significant shift in the use of natural resources. North America and Europe have been the traditional economic power-houses and population centres that demanded a high degree of re-source allocation. Today, the population and economic power shift to cities in Asia, China, Africa, India, and other emerging markets are dictating where natural resources are going.

While that has been good for the economies of Australia, Canada, and other resource-rich nations, it raises questions about future economic prosperity and renewing natural resources. It also brings into question other issues – some local, some national, and some international.

Natural resources form a significant part of Canada's national economy and our international trade. Increasingly, however, the question is being asked: "Have we been good stewards of that land, those natural resources, that bounty given to us?"

The land, the sky, and the water combined to shape our nation. Cities and towns have been built to take advantage of location and access. Land use in Canada tends to be under local municipal dominance and control, or under the jurisdiction of the federal, provincial, or territorial governments that own the vast Crown lands predominant across the country.

The first people to settle the land and to preserve and protect our natural resources were the First Nations. First Nations in Canada (generally) don't control their lands. Under treaty, they are dependent upon government approvals for much of what happens on their territory. Many land claims are before the courts. Ownership of property on reserves is a thorny issue. There is growing unrest within many First Nations about their lack of participation and consultation in proposed northern development projects, ranging from new mines to international pipelines.

## Why the Public Realm Is So Important

A clear understanding of the deep tradition and the importance of the land in our country and culture forms a core foundation of beliefs for many people. This is translated into public policy by all orders of government, supported by the courts and our rule of law.

As individual citizens, we have certain property rights. The state cannot take those away. The state cannot take over private property except under extraordinary conditions. That is how we are governed, and how we allow ourselves to be governed. People have fought and died to protect those core values.

Those values also form much of the relationship we share with our neighbours, and with our community. You can't do things that would negatively impact your neighbours – draining storm water onto someone else's property, for example. We have respect for privacy, and for tolerating what happens on someone else's private property. We may not agree with it, but it is "their land."

But, we are also seeing changes in how generations are living today. The single family in a house in the suburbs is no longer the norm. Cities are building up, not out, and that creates a totally different living environment.

"Fusion neighbourhoods" are replacing traditional ethnic districts. Housing is now accommodating two, three, even four different generations, and often blended families from two or more different cultures. Everything from "granny flats" to multiple kitchens to several separate entrances into a house are becoming more common, as the physical space adapts to the new needs of families.

Conversely, other housing is becoming much smaller as the cost of land rises, and the cost of housing skyrockets – especially in large urban markets. Condos and apartments are shrinking; more people are sharing living space; new social units come together, then break apart.

Virtual strangers can end up sharing accommodations because of financial need, proximity to a workplace, or simply the opportunity to share expenses.

Some have proposed tiny units – some as small as 10'x10', built of recycled materials – as an answer to the growing homeless issue that confronts every city.

The cost of housing has resulted in a startling new trend of micro-homes, some of which can be put together in a week. That means a new era of redesigned home furniture, appliances, and thinking – small scale design of bathrooms, kitchens, fold-away beds, storage space hidden under furniture, sliding partitions, and flip-down desks and tables.

In a number of rapidly growing urban areas, the latest high-rise trend is "micro-suites." These units are 250 to 300 square feet in size. They sell for a significant premium and, on a square footage basis, are highly priced – in Surrey, BC, the price for a 295 square foot unit was $130,000 in 2013.

The larger issue for the residents, however, is where to go to socialize. In a micro-suite (which is roughly a 15' x 20' room), you are not going to be entertaining much. Living space is very limited. It seems unlikely that people will prefer to spend a lot of time in their little boxes.

## The Urban Living Room

That's where the public and private realm collide – the public library, the neighbourhood coffee shop, the Thai restaurant around the corner, the pub with tables on the sidewalk, the park where dogs are walked, the bike path that provides safe cycling along busy streets, the benches under street trees that are becoming community gathering places.

All of a sudden, public places and spaces are becoming the new urban living room. As living spaces diminish, the public realm expands. It is a profound new reality for cities. It will drive more and more public policy in the decades ahead.

This is a crucial answer to another emerging issue – the growing isolation of seniors as our population ages. This is both a social and a health concern. How seniors use the public realm will be quite different from use by highly-connected 20 year-olds; municipalities must plan now for ways to engage single seniors. Cities must become age-friendly communities.

Urban expert Larry Beasley gives an example from Europe: "Local [planning] decisions have a huge day-to-day influence on the quality of how a citizen uses the city, exploits the private economy of the city – a lot more than people think. As we become not only an ideas economy, but an ideas culture, as we communicate in every possible way, it is more important than ever that people can communicate face to face. The public realm becomes where it's happening. In Rotterdam, they've founded the "city lounge" program. It is a clever, contemporary idea."

The urban lounge concept makes the city's core easily accessible, visually appealing, and highly social. It is a quality place where people can come to share food and drink, meet, spend time together, enjoy, and celebrate the public realm. It promotes densification and better use of public spaces. It often involves partnerships with the community and the private sector. City support includes street furniture, design, animating the public realm, and a gentle climate of regulation.

This is a significant paradigm shift in urban planning. Suddenly, cities and their spaces in the public realm are the social venue, the meeting place. As people (especially teens, Gen X and Y, and millenials) increasingly live in a moment-by-moment world of instant communication, municipalities are becoming the social enabler by offering dynamic public places and spaces. It is a new role for cities.

City manager Jeff Fielding understands this new demand for urban sharing. "Man has always wanted to get together, to socialize. We've created places to meet. The most successful cities are the ones that create the stages for people to have those events and opportunities."

Melbourne's Lord Mayor Robert Doyle offers telling proof: "In the inner city, for the first time, restaurants and bars and hospitality places and little grocery outlets overtook the number of retail shops." Melbourne allows tables on sidewalks, which adds to the buzz and activity on the street. It is active socializing. In the electronic communication world of today, it is human relationships that cities must endow. Connectivity.

Architect Jack Diamond picks up on this theme. "At a very fundamental level, human beings need to be part of a society. There is a great deal of satisfaction in being part of a community. Informal contact is as important as formal contact, so the chance encounter is more likely to occur at a crossroads or place that is commonly 'peopled.' The most successful public places are those that you have to go through to get somewhere. Look at the quintessential successful public space: the Italian piazza. They were very well defined by the private sector, with public sector buildings involved. Typically they didn't have empty or open corners. The public space had clear definition, and an inevitability of containment."

"It's the places where you express society," observes Auckland's design champion Ludo Campbell-Reid. "We like people. We like entertainment, we like crowds, we like the buzz, and the public realm is fundamental to that. But, if we are thoughtful about how we design the public realm, there are also places where you can have solitude and time to think. The public realm needs to be quite agile. For me, it's the place where we all come together; that's why it is fundamental [to a great city]."

Toronto planner Jennifer Keesmaat understands this. "What makes a great city are all those places in between – the fabric of the city that we all share in common. It's what connects those buildings where you experience a city, whether it is as a tourist or a resident or just moving about in your daily life."

Focusing on public spaces, she adds, "I believe that, if you strip it all away, it's actually about quality of life, but it's also just about happiness."

Urban experts are becoming persuaded that this is an important but newly-acknowledged role for cities. There is the question, however, of whether politicians understand this role.

As a result, conflict is often arising in municipalities as politicians too often focus on short-term issues for re-election benefits, versus long-term thinking and planning about building great cities. The two aren't usually compatible.

Eddie Friel pulls no punches. "Politicians don't understand that fact. Municipal politicians think in four-year terms. They're not concerned with anything in the first two years except trying to establish themselves, and the next two years they're in election mode. In general, the concern about getting re-elected takes precedence over 'what's the right thing to do'. Having the answer to 'what's the right thing to do' takes total community engagement and having the courage to describe the world as it is, as opposed to the world we would like it to be. If you just keep feeding your community with what they want to hear, and don't provide the leadership that they desperately need in order to survive the challenges of the 21st century knowledge economy, then fundamentally you're being irresponsible."

Indeed, to many citizens today, it feels as if campaigning never stops. There is also concern that the line of separation between governing and campaigning seems to be increasingly blurred. This reality can shift a politician's focus from "how to build a community" to "how to build a war chest for the next campaign." It is a difficult juxtaposition because, when political self-interest is challenged by community needs, too often the public are the losers.

## Rebuilding Our Cities

Politicians don't always appreciate the need for public investments in public space. They don't see the importance of investments in the urban context, and how that translates into economic benefits. Design elements *are* important. Public spaces *are* critical to urban life.

Jennifer Keesmaat faces that all the time. So do urban planners across the country.

"If you're fighting for space, if you're falling off the sidewalk because it isn't wide enough, if the sun is beating down on you because there are no awnings or shade from trees, and there's garbage under foot, that all has a profound impact on how you feel about yourself, how you feel about the space around you. It affects your happiness – whether your life feels pleasure or feels miserable, and that's really the gift of great public spaces. They inspire us. The risk is large scale public disinvestment in any kind of infrastructure. In part, I would argue that we've [often] spent our money in the wrong places in the last generation – we're realizing that we can't afford all of this infrastructure that we have built. We're very skeptical about making large scale infrastructure investments in public spaces," she says candidly.

Billions spent on highways and freeways may not always be returning good value on a livability quotient. Paving more lanes results in more traffic; it is a simple equation. Politicians sometimes don't understand the consequences of a particular decision. Their actions ripple through many segments of our society, and often there are unintended consequences that are exceedingly difficult to fix.

"If you add density without the public spaces that are required to get to that 'happiness factor,' you'll kill the golden goose," says Jennifer Keesmaat firmly.

"There is a big risk that we continue to spend our money in the wrong places. One of the greatest challenges of planning that we face today is being able to shift the emphasis and the recognition to the importance of investing in public infrastructure as being one of the key assets that a city has," she concludes.

The demands of our culture today are totally different from previous generations. Cities need to catch up. Fast.

Those demands also vary. When architect Jack Diamond designed the new city hall in Jerusalem, he understood the unique local tensions and the need for public expression. "We created a public space where protests and gathering could take place. We made it a crossroad and gave it definition. Creating somewhere where people can gather, where you can have concerts, parades, and protests, is critical. It gives focus to community life."

He also understood the growing number of single people and how cities need to give them the opportunity to socialize. "If you look at the most successful public spaces, you could sit at a cafe in the piazza and observe the passage of people. It is no mistake that the

successful cafes are at the upper end, and the walk-through at the
lower end. People-watching is a very important aspect of public life.
You can go there without having to look like you're lonely. That's
the pub in England."

The use of public space, or the intersection of the public and private
realm, are things that a local government can impact and even control. There are strong economic and social benefits for developing a
vibrant public realm, as Larry Beasley knows:

"Cities have to compete with one another. The ambience, experiences, and quality of city are often based on public spaces and places.
The one thing you can [accomplish] that is very impactful for cities
is changing the public realm."

Melbourne, Australia has been chosen for three consecutive years
as the most livable city in the world by the Economist Intelligence
Unit. It is a sophisticated city with an incredible vibe to it. It is also
a city that is vastly different from 25 years ago.

"For a long time, Melbourne was a low density city. We just kept
spreading at the edges," admits the Lord Mayor. "That is not what
a good city does. A thinly spread city lacks vitality. It results in a
car-orientated community. So, we embarked on a program where we
encouraged people to come back into the Central Business District
(CBD) and live here. What's happened is that the density of the core
and immediate surrounding districts has risen. There is much greater
activation in the city – we have about 50 percent of journeys in the
CBD made on foot."

The issue of connectivity through the city has been a critical part in
remaking Melbourne into the dynamic city it is. "[Connectivity] is
one of the great elements of any modern city. It has to be walkable.
It has to be connected. [Melbourne has] the biggest public tram network in the world. We've increased bicycle commuting from two
percent 10 years ago to over 12 percent now. Widened foot paths;
much broader streets than you would normally find in Australian
cities; and an interconnecting series of laneways that also help the
navigability of the city. So, that connectivity of the city that was laid
out, and the proximity of large open spaces, that was the beginning
[of making Melbourne so livable]."

## Urban Chaos

Cities like Melbourne, Copenhagen, Rotterdam, Chicago, and Vancouver are examples of cities that made deliberate decisions to change their planning, urban design, and civic priorities. They have succeeded. It takes time, money, political courage, and a great vision.

The development of cities can also be about destruction. As sad as it is, often a major fire or catastrophe in an older downtown neighbourhood gives rise to bold new development. There is a certain chaos to urban design and development for most communities. Out of destruction comes rebirth. It is how cities use those unique opportunities to enhance their built environment and public and private spaces, and how they intersect, that shapes cities.

The greatest example in recent history was the devastating earthquake that struck Christchurch, New Zealand in 2011. It left 185 dead, half the buildings over five storeys broken or demolished, 10,000 homes red-tagged by officials to prohibit living there, and the closure of its downtown for nearly two years.

It is the largest insurance claim in history, approaching $5B, and will cost $40-50B to repair and rebuild New Zealand's second-largest city. There is a growing sentiment from many locals that the earthquake has offered the city a rare opportunity to reshape itself – perhaps pivoting the downtown to face the river, establishing new precincts for an eco-park, arts and cultural sector, and making Christchurch a great city by the mid-21st century. As one resident commented as we walked along a desolate and barren downtown street, "We have the chance to do it right."

It is an interesting discussion whether massive urban renewal – such as that which Beijing is going through – could have happened in a western democracy. In China, where the state generally owns the land, rights of property "owners" are considerably constricted. Could redevelopment on the scale of the immense rural-to-urban migration in Asia happen as quickly in western cities?

This combination of urban planning chaos, the inability of elected municipal governments to demand higher design standards, and an often scattered and unfocused community plan results in a certain entropy of design and development. The private sector's roles and expectations are ill-defined in many cities.

Finding the right combination of great civic design and raising local expectations are critical tasks for councillors and planners. Unfortunately, the responsibility is too often fumbled because of short-term thinking and a lack of courage to set exacting design standards for the built environment, and to preserve the natural environment.

Those decisions help to shape a city and its reputation – determining whether or not the city appeals to entrepreneurs and people who can drive the local economy, invest in businesses, create clusters of economic successes, and grow and develop talent.

For example, Waterloo, Ontario was the original home of Blackberry when it became a global phenomenon. The city supported the local universities in their commitment to engineering, computers, and technology. Together, the city, university, and private sector created a thriving "tech hub" that encourages innovation and taking research and design to the marketplace. When Blackberry slipped, the rest of the tech industry in the city was strong enough to continue to prosper.

Similarly, when Melbourne lost 25,000 jobs in the automotive manufacturing sector, it replaced them with 50,000 jobs in the creative and knowledge economy.

For cities today, it is all about driving local prosperity, creating economic opportunities for job growth and development, supporting a climate of entrepreneurship, and triumphing in the global hunt for talent.

It is a challenging and difficult time for municipal politicians. They are competing globally for investments, yet it is their decisions locally that determine whether the city that will attract economic opportunities.

Municipalities need great urban planning, bold design, people-centric neighbourhoods, housing that is affordable, public transit that works, and public places and spaces that excite and elevate so they can offer that great quality of life to residents. *That* is the connection to the local prosperity agenda.

# CHAPTER 2

# PLANNING, POLITICS AND PROSPERITY

*"The city as a centre where, any day in any year, there may be a fresh encounter with a new talent, a keen mind or a gifted specialist – this is essential to the life of a country ... a city must be a place where groups of men and women are seeking and developing the highest things they know." – Margaret Mead*

The powerful links between the physical design, structure, and components of a city and its economic strength and job opportunities are frequently misunderstood. When civic leaders fail to connect on this fundamental truth for local government, their community is in jeopardy.

There is a new economy out there, driven by ideas and innovation. Creative thinking. Technology. Using potent new computer tools and concepts. Developing city-to-city international alliances. Encouraging entrepreneurs and small business leaders with a local climate of success and innovation. Supporting the knowledge economy with a community dedicated to life-long learning. Creating regional economic hubs. Seeking niche opportunities. Finding original solutions to a market or industry with a problem. Supporting clusters of bright minds in exciting new job sectors.

Even traditional industries are driven by these new market concepts.

Though it is still facing challenges, General Motors has done a remarkable job of reinventing itself after its near-death experience. It is now exploiting markets in China, shutting down inefficient plants, and adapting robot technology and new manufacturing techniques. The company is better understanding its consumers and then filling their needs with better-built vehicles and improved customer service. It changed its focus: GM is not just in the car-building business, but is competing in the world of mobility. For example, it enables people to operate safely by allowing their communication devices to connect automatically with their vehicles.

Manufacturing isn't about giant, filthy, smoke-spewing buildings. Today, high-tech manufacturing plants use clean processes, intricate supply chains, and robotics. Smart manufacturers are focused on the latest methods and quality controls to produce reliable products. But, they are also using fewer employees, a trend that impacts traditional local economies and employment patterns. Cities need to understand this new reality.

Similarly, natural resource extraction depends on smart engineering, huge trucks and complex equipment, and modern transportation networks to get those products to market (increasingly located in Asia, Africa, and other emerging economies). Smart people are developing a multi-billion dollar resource industry using technology and innovation.

## The CRINK Economy

This new economy goes by several names. The traditional one is "knowledge economy." I find that terminology limiting, however, which is why I coined the phrase "The CRINK Economy" several years ago. It stands for CReative, INnovative, Knowledge-based. Other may refer to this new economy as the smart economy, the creative economy, etc. Perhaps the name is less important than the concept.

What is certain is that economies are being forced to change, often by global forces or national policies over which local politicians have little or no control. Cities that don't adapt to this new business environment risk their community's economic future. This is a critical lesson for municipal politicians and staff. It is not theoretical ... it is the new reality.

Communities that are welcoming and attractive, offering great amenities and a great place to work, are appealing to families. These places are cultured and fun, and have an unrelenting focus on supporting innovation and entrepreneurship. *These* are the communities that will attract talent and money.

Perhaps more simply, it is communities offering a great quality of life that are going to succeed. Jobs and entrepreneurs will be more attracted to them. This link between quality of life and local economic prosperity is unbreakable.

## A Tsunami of Change

Understanding why local economies are failing in some North American cities is a dreadful journey:

New England towns were shuttered as furniture and textile manufacturing disappeared overseas. Older cities in Canada and the U.S. were slaughtered by the "rust belt" realities, when traditional manufacturing changed dramatically (but companies didn't) and jobs left for another jurisdiction. Some municipalities didn't comprehend the shifts in demographics and lifestyle choices, and failed to take proactive measures in time. Corruption and gross political mismanagement permeated too many councils, mayors, and administrations.

History matters less in this tsunami of change than what we can learn from it. The business of today and the opportunities of tomorrow are what civic leaders need to focus on. Strong leadership is needed to ensure future prosperity flows from decisions about what kind of community to create, how to attract people, and how to best develop the public realm.

It is a vastly different environment in which cities operate today.

International expert Eddie Friel offers a clear perspective. "Places and cities and towns are about people first. It's not about buildings; it's about people and why a group of people chose to live and bring up their families in a particular place. The nature of work in the 21st century knowledge economy is moving the goalposts for municipalities.

"In the global economy, places have to be able to define themselves in terms of what they have that somebody else wants to purchase. That's a very strange situation for [cities] to be in because it means we're now in a marketplace. How can a community suddenly find itself in a marketplace? Because the unit of analysis for performance in this knowledge economy is the city-region."

This larger, regional thinking signals a big change for economic and political planning. Global forces are increasingly at play in local economies, as Eddie Friel acknowledges: "It was fine in the past when nations could control their economies and their capital. That control is now gone. There are no boundaries any more. That creates a whole new set of questions for communities, for city-regions and how you define them: what the assets are, and how you generate wealth for everybody in that city-region. That is a whole new range of enormous challenges to legislators and to communities themselves who have to rethink what they're doing and how they're doing it. Who will their communities be 25 years from now?"

This question is fundamental to civic planning today, as municipalities wrestle with diminishing budgets, growing demands, and increasing international competition for talent and investment. It is also a key reason why local politicians need to better understand and appreciate global trends, policies, practices, and development.

Making the community more competitive should drive the agenda. The legacy for municipal councils is increasingly dependent on the economic prosperity, cultural opportunities, social stability, and environmental sustainability. These four pillars of smart municipal growth are critical. Great civic planning and urban design is a thread that runs through all of them.

That doesn't mean paving over every green space in the name of new development. In fact, it means quite the opposite. It means building smart, livable cities that offer a great quality of life.

Millions of hours and even more millions of dollars have been wasted by pontificating politicians trying to answer the question that Eddie Friel raised: Who does your city want to be in 25 years? Simplistic efforts to "re-brand" cities with fancy, consultant-invented, made-up slogans with the hope that it solves all their problems won't work.

If you don't have an attractive, sustainable, warm, and family-friendly city that offers that great quality of life, the most fantastic slogan in the world won't deliver results. You need to have the product before you can market it. That means a city needs to commit unswervingly to building a more livable community and encouraging local innovation.

As Bruce Katz and Julie Wagner (of the Brooking Institution in Washington, DC) wrote on the Quartz news website, "Talented people want to work and live in urban places that are walkable, bikeable, connected by transit, and hyper-caffeinated. Major companies across multiple sectors are practising 'open innovation' and want to be close to other firms, research labs, and universities. Entrepreneurs want to start their companies in collaborative spaces, where they can share ideas and have efficient access to everything from legal advice to sophisticated lab equipment."

A clear-eyed understanding of the necessary decision making and analysis is critical for moving communities forward in the competitive global economic environment.

Larry Beasley is adamant about applying this tough new way of thinking to local decision making about urban design and building strong cities. "We need to frame this not in terms of culture and aesthetics, but in terms of economic development and prosperity. Do you want your city to be competitive with other cities to attract capital, intelligence, and other things that create the economy of your city?"

This new paradigm uses analytics, metrics, and careful, honest examination of a city and its future. It looks for fresh ideas without the constriction of traditional thinking. Finding answers can be hard when the questions are wrong, or where there is a lack of honesty about the realities of the problem.

These are big, difficult questions. Turning around a local economy is hard. It takes time, money, a strong strategic plan, and the courage to stay on course. It takes dedication.

While the answers vary with every community, there are some common elements – strong leadership is one of the keys.

## Making Great Cities

The McKinsey Global Institute, in its 2013 report *How to Make a City Great*, argues that leaders who make important strides in improving their cities do those three things really well:

> **They achieve smart growth.** *Smart growth identifies and nurtures the very best opportunities for growth, plans ways to cope with its demands, integrates environmental thinking, and ensures that all citizens enjoy a city's prosperity. Good city leaders also think about regional growth because as a metropolis expands, they will need the cooperation of surrounding municipalities and regional service providers. Integrating the environment into economic decision making is vital to smart growth: cities must invest in infrastructure that reduces emissions, waste production, and water use, as well as in building high-density communities.*
>
> **They do more with less.** *Great cities secure all revenues due, explore investment partnerships, embrace technology, make organizational changes that eliminate overlapping roles, and manage expenses. Successful city leaders have also learned that, if designed and executed well, private-public partnerships can be an essential element of smart growth, delivering lower-cost, higher-quality infrastructure and services.*
>
> **They win support for change.** *Change is not easy, and its momentum can even attract opposition. Successful city leaders build a high-performing team of civil servants, create a working environment where all employees are accountable for their actions, and take every opportunity to forge a stakeholder consensus with the local population and business community. They take steps to recruit and retain top talent, emphasize collaboration, and train civil servants in the use of technology.*
>
> *Mayors are only too aware that their tenure will be limited. But, if longer-term plans are articulated – and gain popular support because of short-term successes – leaders can start a virtuous cycle that sustains and encourages a great urban environment.*

(Shannon Bouton, David Cis, Lenny Mendonca, Herbert Pohl, Jaana Remes, Henry Ritchie, Jonathan Woetzel, "How to Make a City Great," McKinsey & Company, <www.mckinsey.com/insights>, September 2013.)

This kind of "big thinking" is too often missing at the local government level. Governments in North America are often fixated on the next election cycle, not generational-change opportunities and strategies. Understanding massive shifts in demographic cycles, or global economic strategies and investments, or the movement of people and resources in far-away nations are rarely the focus of elected officials. But, it is those changes – be they subtle or seismic – that lead, over time, to the closing of local manufacturing plants, the shift of the workforce, and ultimately the despair of a sinking community.

Long-term thinking results in the discovery of important new medical research, the reallocation of global resources to hot new economies, or the latest technological advances generating new opportunity and job categories for a community.

Too often, elected officials today become small thinkers doing small things. It is a great weakness in our system. Visionary leadership is often missing in municipalities ... in government period.

There is frequently tension between staff and elected officials over big questions and decisions. There is often mistrust between trained professionals in a field, and those elected by the people to make decisions about their community's future.

To some extent, urban planners share the blame for the problems. The economic foundation got lost. The links between prosperity, jobs, great public places and spaces, attractive quality of life amenities, and strong urban design and planning broke down.

As Jennifer Keesmaat very honestly admits, "As a profession, we've gone through a really bad period where we lost our way. We actually allowed this false paradigm of market demand to shape our planning outcomes, instead of going back to first principles of great urbanism, great design, what's viable from an economic development perspective, what's imperative from a health/culture perspective. We lost our way in terms of using those lenses, and using overall quality of life and sustainability as being the key drivers to creating great places. We planned a lot of stuff that doesn't really work very well. We need to take more ownership and responsibility for that. A lot of the congestion problems, the decay we see in suburbs today, that was poor planning."

The tasks of seeking superior local planning decisions, enhancing the community's quality of life, and supporting and building jobs and local prosperity are closely entwined. With the often dramatic changes in a community's economic base, that also translates into changes in the local housing market – where people want to live, how they get to work, where they want to socialize, and where and how they play with their families. Again, we see the vital importance of the public realm and how citizens are using it.

Cities that invest wisely in public places and spaces are more likely to attract people and jobs. Cities that decline precipitously and lose focus, that ignore the public realm and the needs of their citizens, quickly fall into that downward spiral that is so difficult to reverse.

A few years ago, the U.S. Gallup organization completed a three-year project that interviewed 46,000 people in large and small cities across America. They were interested in how people became engaged with their local community and invested in its success. In other words, can the attachment of residents to their community increase that city's GDP and economic prosperity? The answer was a clear, "Yes."

The reasons, however, may surprise.

To summarize this very important report, Gallup found the top three drivers for local engagement and support were:

1.  Social comfort – places where people can meet and socialize, sports, entertainment, art, vibrant nightlife ...

2.  Acceptance – the city should make you feel safe and comfortable, welcoming to all residents, with a diverse population ...

3.  Aesthetics – an attractive city offering parks, green spaces, public art, tree-lined streets, safe trails and pathways ...

*People drive strong local economies, so how cities attract and retain entrepreneurs and graduates by creating vibrant, people-oriented public places is critical in the global hunt for talent. Sydney Harbour, above, provides a great example of the animated public space.*

How cities develop, protect, and support the public realm has a direct correlation to citizen attraction to and satisfaction with their local community.

Increasingly relevant to cities, attracting the talent means attracting good jobs. This is the critical link that many in government don't get.

The scenarios are common: A government (at any level) proudly announces another round of cost-cutting "to save hard-working families from being over-taxed and over-burdened." They cut investments in culture, or architecture, or supporting local parks and libraries, or providing great public spaces where people can meet and socialize. The result is the paradox of planning: They create exactly the *opposite* effect on their local economy, compared to what they want.

Architect Jack Diamond has built projects around the world, and understands this connection between prosperous cities and happy

residents. "The importance of quality of life, which is actually
counterintuitive, is best for the economy. Cultural facilities, security,
quality of housing, neighbourhoods, where the trees are ... often the
difference between great suburbs and not great is the maturity of the
trees and where they're placed."

Politicians and planners need to grasp this concept. In the global
battle for attracting investments, entrepreneurs, talent, technology,
and prosperity, what you do at the local level matters. A lot. Planning decisions are crucial. What goes on in neighbourhoods is important. How clean the streets and sidewalks are downtown sends a
message. Where do people go to meet and interact?

## Does your public realm support your economic model?

Here are two basic questions local government officials need to ask:

1.  Is your city's public realm supporting your community's
    economic model?

2.  Is your city plan supporting your community's economic
    model?

Sometimes, the best economic development strategy isn't to run
around frantically trying to bag an elephant; it may be much more
productive to clean up the city, green it, improve the quality of life,
and provide a great environment for people to enjoy.

The reason is simple – most of your economic development will
come from the growth and expansion of the small and medium-
sized businesses that are already in your community. Too many
councils forget that, and never even acknowledge or thank their local businesses.

Doing simple things – like eliminating the bureaucratic problems of
dealing with city hall – are productive accomplishments for council.
Do you want to roll out the red tape, or the red carpet?

You need to look at your town or city through fresh eyes. Are your
zoning by-laws and planning policies supporting the needs of local
business? Are you delivering an attractive city? Do your policies at
city hall reward innovation and creativity – inside and outside city

hall? Are your planning policies and decisions allowing business to do business? Are community interests and neighbourhood needs part of your focus? Does city hall provide answers promptly and accurately?

It is now clearly established that great cities attract great people, who get great jobs, and therefore support a strong economy. If any of those links in the economic chain are broken, the formula breaks down.

Government officials need to grasp these monumental changes, because they relate directly to local planning policies and decisions. Cities need to understand their market and their customers:

➤ how and where people live;

➤ too many families living in fear instead of hope, with nearly 50 percent of families living paycheque-to-paycheque;

➤ public transportation planning and accessibility;

➤ the fear of many young people that they will never own their own home, so how do we make housing more affordable;

➤ how suburban life is changing and how it needs to be replenished;

➤ the push to build up, not out – and how condo living is changing urban society;

➤ the health issues impacted by planning policies and decisions – everything from childhood obesity to the increase in diabetes;

➤ sustainability concerns and how communities can lead the path for change.

There is growing discontent about the commuting lifestyle, yet urban areas keep pushing deeper into suburban and exurban regions. Commuting takes a toll on the health of residents, and the impact on the environment is undeniable. It also has a large economic cost – billions of dollars annually.

There are fascinating new trends beginning to emerge:

➤ Fewer young people brought up in metro regions own a vehicle
   or even have a driver's licence. What will that mean for transportation planning in the future?

➤ How much will new technologies and devices impact where
   and how people do their work? Will telecommuting become
   more predominant? What will that mean to big, people-stuffed
   buildings downtown?

➤ There are growing commitments to sustainability. Will planning
   and zoning regulations of the future demand green roofs, green
   walls, use of greywater, self-contained heating and cooling
   units?

➤ M2M (machine to machine) technology is poised to revolution-
   ize day-to-day living. We can build smarter buildings, where
   computers will monitor everything from temperature to security
   to fire – and take action without human intervention.

➤ Is there a gigantic switch starting to happen, because of commuting and lifestyle issues, where the suburbs become the en-
   clave of the poor, and the rich return to downtown urban housing?

Society is changing, often rapidly. We are becoming more diverse,
more tolerant, more accepting of different lifestyles. That, too,
is impacting our lives and our neighbourhoods. Immigration is
changing the face of many communities.

The links between planning, prosperity, and politics are crystal
clear. Cities need to ensure that their planning policies and practices
lead these changes. Only being reactive is a sign of poor local government policy and analysis. Leadership is paramount.

Meanwhile, there is another monumental change blinking urgently
on our radar screens: Cities are seeing a new/old reality emerge –
increasingly, people want to live where they work.

# CHAPTER 3

# LIVE WHERE YOU WORK

*"Cities are gentrified by the following types of people in sequence: first, the risk-oblivious (artists), then the risk-aware (developers), finally the risk adverse (dentists from New Jersey)."* – Bill Kraus

Jobs. Jobs for young people. It has emerged as perhaps the biggest issue following the world's gradual recovery from the 2008/2009 meltdown.

"Generation Screwed" is what some students and young people call themselves today. They see little hope of finding a job, let alone a good job. University degrees suddenly don't guarantee a comfortable future. Baby boomers, many of whom have seen their jobs and financial security leached away, are staying in the workforce longer. "Freedom 55" is now just a bitter memory.

Seniors are becoming wealthier from real estate booms and inheritances from frugal parents, even as they qualify for a wide variety of discounts, ranging from bus passes to banking fees. At the same time, some young people and families starting out are much more financially vulnerable, saddled with student loan repayments, diminished future pension plans, and fierce competition for jobs.

The "middle class" is being squeezed and, for many, is under attack. Pensions, other than for government and public service jobs, have been eroded or eliminated. Salaries are not increasing much. Trying to break into the job market is hard. Stories of PhDs driving taxis or tending bar are rampant. The cost of food, energy, communications, and other utilities keeps jumping. Young families face high costs for daycare and child-rearing expenses.

As birth rates decline in western nations, immigration becomes both a solution and a challenge. Will provinces and states recognize foreign credentials? Will there be language barriers? How do employers fill the job-gap while complaining they can't find qualified workers – even as some cities suffer record unemployment?

## Marketplace Shifts

There are basic shifts occurring in the marketplace. The demand for skilled trades is rising, at the same time as many old-world craftspeople are retiring. The old-fashioned apprenticeship/mentoring programs are now seen by many as inefficient and slow. The resource industries can be an economic roller-coaster for those employed in the sector and for the municipalities that are their homes. Communities are scrambling to draw jobs in the CRINK economy.

Attracting skilled workers can be difficult. There are growing concerns that Canada isn't producing enough engineers, technology experts, and math and science graduates. Math test results for Canadian students have plummeted. There is an overall need to bring more innovation and technology to a marketplace that is at-risk without these skill sets.

The job and marketplace realities must be acknowledged by municipalities. It is this new and different foundation of jobs and economic investment that changes communities.

For example, when a mine is discovered or an oil field opened, the impact on the local community is enormous and unrelenting. The municipality is almost always completely unprepared for what is about to happen. They don't have the infrastructure in place, sufficient zoned and serviced land for housing, or the capacity to handle the sudden impact. Council and staff are overwhelmed. Often, the provincial or state government is slow to respond to the demands for growth, serviced land, and housing needs, so market forces drive bad planning decisions – the outcomes of which linger for years.

Communities in northern Alberta, southern Saskatchewan, and North and South Dakota have exploded with temporary camps, make-shift housing, and soaring prices as shale oil discoveries sud-

Chapter 3 • LIVE WHERE YOU WORK

denly drive local economies. A host community is changed forever. "Temporary" planning decisions become permanent fixtures.

These well-paid new jobs disrupt families and typically see employees traveling thousands of miles for work. Yet, ironically, companies in boom towns often desperately search for qualified employees. The job market is shifting quickly. It is very difficult for towns and cities to anticipate growth demands or sudden plant closings – and almost impossible to keep up with future demands.

Meanwhile, artificial intelligence, the new economy, globalization, robotics, automation, technology, and other advances are changing the traditional industrial base. The result is fewer jobs in factories and a massive workforce that needs retraining and often relocating. That, too, changes a host community.

## Housing and Work Choices

*A young couple returns from working in Asia. They eschew suburban life for a downtown urban home. What makes their choice particularly interesting is that they have two young children. They deliberately chose a dense urban environment in which to raise their family.*

In metro and large urban areas, the influx of creative minds, immigration patterns, and a steady increase in CRINK economy jobs is changing how people live in large urban areas. Condos and apartments are getting smaller at the same time as the buildings are getting higher. That means new and very different patterns on the street, changes in public transportation, new uses of the public realm, and changes in how people socialize and communicate.

In municipalities of any size, there are significant shifts going on because of the changes in the job market and the workforce. Municipalities are often caught unaware of the trends and patterns (or have ignored them) and are thus slow or unprepared to respond.

If older cities become hollowed-out, they can quickly fall into a grim downward spiral. Often, neighbourhoods or cities need to hit bottom before a concerted, focused energy begins to revive the community. Sometimes, that effort comes too late – or it is too hard, and too expensive. The risk-adverse are horrified.

Municipalities need to better understand the marketplace, demographic shifts, workplace demands, and how families and workers are requiring different ways of living. They need to be thinking about new ways of shaping and building our communities and how people live in them.

## Live Where You Work

More and more people share one common reality: they are living closer to where they work.

"One of the most important things from a planning perspective around sustainability is ensuring that people can choose to live near where they work. When we poll people about why they live downtown, it is because they can walk to work, or transit or cycle. The carbon footprint of those choosing to live downtown is significantly lower than anyone else in the GTA," says Jennifer Keessmaat.

In some ways, this is a return to the lifestyle of a century ago. It simply made sense to live where you worked because no one had cars, and public transportation was very limited. Thus, gritty little houses appeared close to shipyards and factories, and neighbourhoods grew near industrial areas.

It took the emergence of streetcars to provide a path out for families. Suddenly, you could live a short public transit-ride away from where you worked or shopped in the downtown. Families got a bit of lawn, and what became ethnic-dominated neighbourhoods emerged, tethered to the church and school. Butchers and bakers sprung up. A police officer walked the streets, knew the kids, and kept order with the odd cuff on the backside and a lot of common sense. Kids played outside, inventing their own games, and returning home when they were hungry or bleeding. Mothers kept an eye on the street while running the house, and dad returned at night from a hard day's work to a hot supper.

*The Mag-Lev train in Shanghai travels over 400 kms/hr, and is part of the modern infrastructure investments that have helped to drive China's strong economy*

Jack Diamond acknowledges this evolution: "Originally, it was the streetcar subdivision – public transit went out in an orderly grid, which allowed the first migration out of the urban centre. This whole issue of living remotely from where you work is a very modern concept."

That desire burst out with the suburban revolution of the post-World War II era. The driving force was simple: automobiles. Families could move out of an urban tenement environment, stretch beyond the limits of the streetcar, and own their own home. It came complete with a tree, grass, sometimes a swimming pool in the backyard, and, for sure, a shiny, chrome-laden car in the garage that dad and the kids washed and polished regularly.

Cities responded by building roads – lots of roads. As it became easier to travel on those roads, more cars were sold, more families moved to the suburbs, demand for more roads increased, and cities responded by building freeways and tangles of overpasses that led to more freeways.

That changed the face of North American cities. It also began a distinctive separation from traditional European cities, which have tended to remain more urban-centric – apartments downtown, walkable neighbourhoods, piazzas and public meeting places, and daily shopping for food.

In Canada and the U.S., life was changed by suburban shopping centres and super-highways. Freeways sometimes cut through traditional downtown neighbourhoods, hastening and exacerbating the hollowing-out of urban cores. This exodus to the suburbs paralyzed much municipal planning and thinking. Some terrible things were done – streets with no sidewalks, neighbourhoods with no street lights, cul-de-sacs everywhere.

Municipal planning became focused on the needs of the car. There was a fundamental shift from developing neighbourhoods for people to serving the needs of vehicles. Councils became enthralled with developers promising to pave over those useless green spaces around the city; new developments sprung up. Everywhere. "Bulldoze those old trees, we'll plant shrubs in the front yard." Sure, sign here.

People were living far away from where they worked, and demands for public transit began to get louder. Commuters became a new breed, often travelling an hour, then two, to get to their jobs.

In the 60s and early 70s, federal and provincial governments were flush with cash and often paid significant portions of the cost for new roads and highways for cities. Suburbs kept pushing out. Brand new cities began to emerge from what was once farmland or distant commercial uses.

Larry Beasley knows that history. "A lot of mistakes were made 50 years ago. The creative culture of urbanism was very strong up until the 1930s. It was diluted – polluted by modern architecture philosophy that got translated into brutalism that was so popular after the war. Then, it was taken over by people who believed in the incredible benefits of the car. Streets got twice as big. From that time, in every year in every city I know of, more and more space was pulled away from the public to more comfortably accommodate the car agenda. Starting in the 1980s, 90s, people are trying to reclaim [public] space."

It was a planning debacle that struck cities in many parts of the globe. For Auckland, Ludo Campbell-Reid is clear on the culprit: "Auckland was quite an intense European-designed city, including a wonderful tramway system that was ripped up in 1956. The motorcar took over. That's the time that Auckland turned a corner; it turned into a different city. This is a place where people fell out of love with their city."

It is a stunning admission. *People fell out of love with their city.* Could there be a more damning indictment for planners and politicians?

Today, commuters are realizing the downside of a suburban/commuting lifestyle. Unproductive hours spent alone in a car. Frustration at gridlock and traffic jams. The cost of building and maintaining super-highways. The cost to the environment from millions of cars idling in stop-and-go traffic jams. An exhausting lifestyle. An unsustainable model.

"The GO Train is only a more efficient expressway," says Jack Diamond. "[The suburban growth concept] is unaffordable from the public policy standpoint. For every dollar you get in tax, it costs you $1.40 to service. We have subsidized developers because they don't pay the incremental costs (for subways and expressways). That's what created the suburbs. It has provided complete subservience to the automobile. The provincial governments are the ones that [have allowed this]. We don't have planning; what determines our subways are the sewer systems. If you look at the trunk lines and highways, that's where we have development. The answer to this is full-cost pricing. If every house had to pay its share of the capital investment in the public infrastructure, you'd have a very different outcome."

"Planners did some terrible things – no sidewalks, no connectivity, car-focused, lack of trees and green space," comments John Nicholson on bad suburban design. "Your backyard can be on the back of something else, but you can't get there without driving a mile and half. It just doesn't make sense."

## Feet on the Street

Inevitably, we are seeing a return to the work/life style of a century ago – once again, people want to live near where they work. Families are trying desperately to find time together. More people want off the treadmill.

That has resulted in a change of focus for urban design and development for the past couple of decades, as communities try to regain the vibe and energy of an active, attractive downtown core.

"I think what's happening now is a reversal of that [suburban lifestyle]. Urban condo influx is a terrific demonstration of that desire to walk to work, bike to work, short streetcar ride to work," says Jack Diamond.

Most cities believe that more people living downtown will result in a more vibrant downtown. It will spark interesting little cafés and coffee shops, retailers, and restaurants. There is a certain safety and security in numbers. People on the sidewalk are a sign of a healthy downtown.

Greater density is the benefit. The services are already in place for new downtown high-rise projects, so the city's costs are minimal, yet such projects generate huge development charges. Higher density means more feet on the street. It can also provide a new opportunity to reshape the public realm and encourage interesting urban design innovations.

"We've tried to have mixed use in the city," says Melbourne's Robert Doyle. "When you combine that with density, that to me is what creates vibrancy. Everything a citizen needs to find or experience is within easy walking distance in the core. It is more efficient, but it is also more sustainable and more socially inclusive."

Buildings to accommodate this influx are undergoing new thinking by architects and developers. There is greater awareness of the need to gently link high-rise buildings with the street. Cities are beginning to ask for appealing design elements in these buildings – things like set-backs, tapered design of upper floors to reduce the shadowing and footprint, and a mix of retail and commercial sites to provide an interactive on-street presence.

Robert Doyle is clear about Melbourne's urban design standards: "We are much more interested in what happens when a building hits the sidewalk than we are in the building itself. It has to have an active frontage to the street. We prefer podium-style buildings so there is a human scale to the architecture. We protect the best of our [heritage] architecture and we develop the rest, but we don't seek to protect everything."

Architects are finding interesting uses for physical materials – glass, public art, water features, and creating new public space as part of the complex.

For example, Vancouver has traditionally demanded much of its developers, and in return has used private money to build beautiful public spaces. Gently-flowing water features and green spaces designed around the entrances and as part of the surrounding space of the high-rise are now routinely used as the developer's contribution to making the city so attractive and livable.

Setting these parameters and expectations is the job of the municipality, and is generally referred to as "placemaking." It may be defined as: *"An urban design process to create neighbourhoods with a distinct character."*

Some of the key principles of placemaking include:

➤ healthy lifestyles;

➤ green initiatives;

➤ innovative housing and social mix;

➤ protection of natural features, rather than encouraging bulldozers;

➤ pedestrian focused and public-transit friendly;

➤ strong sense of community; and

➤ high quality public spaces and public art.

Some of this new thinking about the importance of places and spaces has been sparked in recent years by an increased focus on cultural planning, which recognizes the importance of linking a community's cultural/artistic/heritage assets with its economic opportunities and its urban design/growth policies and expectations.

Many progressive municipalities understand that a cultural plan can provide an important opportunity to do some re-thinking about their community and its design. There are many reasons to support the cultural planning process, but the top 10 are:

1. Fresh new vision for the community.

2. Revitalization of neighbourhoods.

3. Furthering a "sense of place."

4. Generating new economic opportunities.

5. Livelier streets and neighbourhoods.

6. Innovative urban design and street action.

7. Link between education, community, and development.

8. Support for children's arts/cultural experiences.

9. More appealing community for creative sector, economic investments, local food, and tourists.

10. Greener, more livable and sustainable community.

These elements join urban design for a re-focused effort by the community to develop its own distinctive aesthetic reputation that can attract talent and investment.

## Downtown Revitalization

There isn't a city around that doesn't want a robust downtown. There are a number of key elements to rejuvenating a moribund district, including:

➤ arts and heritage facilities;

➤ strong cultural assets;

➤ artisans and artists, who often lead the renaissance;

➤ food and fun;

➤ strong commercial presence, with a variety of businesses and opportunities;

➤ residential development that is mixed-use and connects with the street;

➤ cultural and culinary tourism opportunities;

➤ abundant retail and business outlets (people hate dark, closed buildings);

➤ walkable/bike-friendly streets;

➤ safe, welcoming, clean, green, attractive street furniture;

➤ performance venues; and

➤ unique experiences.

These core attributes support a dynamic neighbourhood – and too many planners and politicians forget that a downtown is also a neighbourhood. A big central library may serve the entire city, but it is also the branch library for that neighbourhood.

There is a growing concern about gentrification of dis-spirited older urban neighbourhoods. Once the creative sector has made an area "cool" (or hot), it gets discovered by trendsetters and the media, and is then invaded by developers with money. Prices rise; artisans get squeezed out; interesting buildings get a boring face-lift; and, too often, the unique vibe from the artistic community gets lost.

Municipal governments have the opportunity to re-shape neighbourhoods and revitalize districts through smart design elements, protecting heritage in the area, setting high expectations for urban design, and supporting innovative residential and commercial concepts.

Whether in small towns or large cities, there are strong similarities in what people want in a vibrant downtown. This is also important politically, as many residents – fairly or unfairly – judge a community's health primarily on the state of the downtown.

Tourists and visitors are instinctively attracted to the downtown core. In most downtowns, they know they will find decent hotels, good restaurants, tourist information, a central library, and a certain sense of security. Having a great downtown is really important for strong communities.

What people want from a downtown (indeed, what visitors want from a city) are great experiences. A community that can't deliver on those expectations is not going to succeed in the highly competitive (and lucrative) tourist economy. This is another key reason why investing in the community, supporting a strong downtown, demanding a high degree of art and culture, and providing great public places and spaces is not only a community benefit – it is part of a smart municipal council's economic development and prosperity agenda.

All of these pieces fit together to build an interesting and exciting downtown. That is what urban residents want, and that is how cities will get more "feet on the street."

It is a symbiotic process for urban planners, developers, and architects; for visionaries and hard-nosed business investors; and for municipal councillors.

And, as evidenced in metro areas around the world, the building pattern is *up,* not *out.*

## Reaching for the Sky

The world's tallest building is the Burj Khalifa. It stands a towering 160 storeys and is the centrepiece of downtown Dubai, offering a stunning array of hotel, commercial, and living spaces.

The Shanghai World Financial Centre features 101 storeys to accommodate its offices and hotel space.

A new skyscraper in Manhattan is being touted as the world's tallest residential building. It will soar 96 storeys.

Western Europe's tallest building is The Shard in London – a mere 72 storeys.

One of the ways cities can increase density is to allow developers to build up. Many cities also use that policy to extract additional (and often significant) community benefits for that added density. It may come from cash fees, elevated design techniques, or demands for public spaces. It may create urban green space or other benefits.

The giant towers are a mixed blessing for cities. They enhance the use of public transit, but also place significant demand on the transportation system. They increase density and population in that neighbourhood; but, while they pay large amounts in property taxes to city coffers, they also increase demand on infrastructure including local utilities. Then, there is the impact on sidewalk traffic flows and the potential effect from shadowing, wind, and other considerations on the existing streetscape.

Bold design is critical in such projects. There is a strong push for mixed-use components, particularly a retail/commercial street presence that takes the building out to the people, rather than creating an impenetrable barrier between the building and the street.

This concept has been common in Asian cities, where land is so valuable that there can be many floors of commercial use. It isn't unusual to see a restaurant – something North Americans traditionally expect as a ground-floor use – on the fourth or fifth floor of a building in Hong Kong.

Some buildings offer retail on the street level, commercial on the next few floors, then hotel, then residential. Guests are sometimes surprised that a hotel reception desk can be on the 23rd floor. It is a different way of thinking about urban design and what makes up the street presence.

While many of the newest skyscrapers are pyramid-like in design, rising to a far-away point, there is also a trend to curvature in the design. Among the best-known recently are the Absolute Towers in Mississauga, Ontario, which won an international design competition in 2013. The graceful curves of the condo building (nicknamed the "Marilyn Monroe Towers," after the famous actress) offer innovative design and an eye-catching presence.

Municipal leaders need to be open to new ways of thinking, and must pay careful attention to the proposed development of buildings and projects – including the impact on the existing neighbourhood. They need to better grasp the needs of developers at the same time as fully understanding the demands and availability of servicing and infrastructure.

Planning decisions have become much more complex. Local government officials, both elected and administrative, are under greater pressure to make the right decisions – and the perception of what is "right" can vary considerably throughout a community.

Handling development issues is a core responsibility for municipalities. Architect John Nicholson deals with many local governments and their policies. He believes that public officials need to do "anticipatory work ... that is, set design guidelines and parameters around which intensification or new development is put forward. For example, if NIMBY is not addressed in anticipation of that development, then I think you're setting it up for conflict, if not failure."

City manager Jeff Fielding understands the constant battle over urban design. "People don't want to be told what they can or cannot build. The difficulty is the city can't become the design police, instead of facilitating creative design."

Too often, this conflict between local government policies and by-laws, an often indifferent or indecisive council, and a lack of confidence in demands to elevate expectations for design results in mediocre, uninspired projects that fail to excite the community. Developers sometimes need to be pushed; but municipal officials are often scared to do the pushing.

It takes courage and confidence for a municipality to set urban design guidelines and raise the bar for architects and developers. Municipal councils frequently crumble under questions or demands that some see as threats ("if council doesn't approve this application, we'll take the project down the road to _____").

It also means the community must have a strong sense of its own values, and a broadly-accepted vision for its growth and design. This strikes at the heart of the relationship between local government and the business/development community. Many times, the municipality is seen as nothing more than an impediment, enforcing rules that are confusing, ridiculous, out of date, and unfair.

"[New Zealand has] a very tightly run planning system. Quite legalistic, quite adversarial. It tells you what you can and can't do here.

But, there is no real prescription around design, so that's left to the power of negotiation," acknowledges Ludo Campbell-Reid, Auckland's urban design champion.

In many countries, the planning and the urban design departments are separate. Statutory planners are interested in the rules, while designers are interested in aesthetics, design, and the connection with the street. Generally, designers have the upper hand. Councils, however, have the final say.

"Sometimes, you can't [get private sector buy-in] and we just regulate them," says Robert Doyle. But, the private sector in Melbourne has also figured out that if they work with the planning department and the urban design department, right from the early concepts, they can work out projects.

How can we be innovative and creative when the city doesn't have contemporary regulations and a vision that works? That's a question that many developers are asking.

It is a reasonable point. Jennifer Keesmaat faces the conflict every day.

"Planners often get blamed for political decisions," she states accurately. But, she also accepts responsibility for some failings by planning officials. "Planners need to connect with neighbourhoods in a stronger, more unified voice. Build credibility. Due diligence. Have a deep sense of responsibility to the public interest."

"There is disconnect between planners and elected officials," She says. "Planners are regulatory. As planners, we need to figure out the outcomes. The rules are changing because the rules don't make sense if they aren't creating a great city. What is the city seeking to achieve? Rules can be a friend, but not if they are giving bad outcomes ... we need to change the conversation, new ways of thinking, dealing with various publics," she admits candidly.

Rules. Regulations. Policies. By-laws. Development conditions. Zoning restrictions. Urban design demands.

How do municipalities start/continue to encourage great urban design of their towns and cities?

How do designers and developers get on board with the local government?

And, how do municipalities, designers, and developers support employees who more and more want to live where they work?

Great architecture can provide an image that results in an iconic global brand for a community and a greatly elevated national and international profile.

# CHAPTER 4

# THE DNA OF YOUR CITY

*"The city is not a concrete jungle, it is a
human zoo." – Desmond Morris*

The Opera House in Sydney. The Golden Gate Bridge in San Francisco. The Eiffel Tower in Paris.

As Hollywood movie directors have known for generations, simply flashing a quick picture of any of these landmarks instantly identifies the location for the audience. No words or titles are necessary. They are iconic – the incontrovertible symbol of that city, an image that is clear and highly recognizable.

Marvellous design elements form a community's distinctive identity. These become the personality of your city or town. They quickly shape your image and what people around the world will come to know about your community. The physical realm – the public and private spaces and places, the vibrancy of the street, the creativity of local architecture, and the respect for heritage properties and the natural environment in and around the city – combine to form your civic DNA.

These "bones" that comprise civic infrastructure are the core and foundation for what we need to build, strengthen, and evolve in competitive 21st century cities and towns.

New, innovative projects are not always instantly supported by the community, of course (Gustave Eiffel was vilified when the tower was first presented.)

The design concept for the Sydney Opera House was plucked from the reject pile by a late-arriving member of the judging panel; construction was a long, expensive, and torturous path. (The architect got dumped and never saw his finished masterpiece.)

Encouraging, demanding, bold urban design requires intrepid civic leaders.

How citizens experience a city says much about that community. A sun-dappled street, alive with trees and people. The buzz of a vibrant urban plaza as the subway pulls in. A gleaming tower with spectacular new design and building materials to enchant its tenants. A calm, green oasis in the middle of a busy neighbourhood. These are the things that shape a city and our passion for that community.

It is the public realm. It is our public places and spaces. It is the private realm. It is where the two collide. It is our urban adventure. It is urban life today.

## Shaping the City

Tall buildings have come to symbolize modern urban life. They use space efficiently. They influence the street and the neighbourhood in how they connect with the sidewalk. Their design increasingly reflects human scale. These skyscrapers can also offer a poetic symbol for a city, where magnificent design meets civic ambition.

Architect Louis Sullivan perhaps set the standard when talking about the design and importance of skyscrapers, proclaiming, "It must be every inch a proud and soaring thing, rising in sheer exultation." He said that in 1896.

Since then, more often than not, buildings have disappointed. They have failed to reach the standards of a "proud and soaring thing." Often, local governments have been accountable for delivering grey, boring, concrete boxes to their communities.

Too often, architects hide behind "context" to defend their boring designs. And, municipalities too often fail to set high standards and expectations for creative and innovative concepts.

Great architecture creates beauty for the eye and for the soul. It can transform a district or a neighbourhood. It inspires, leads, immerses one in pleasure. It can even help heal, as people are discovering after the opening of the expanded St. Mary's Hospital in Sechelt, on BC's Sunshine Coast. Using traditional bent wood cedar design from the First Nations in the region, the health care facility offers arguably the greenest hospital in Canada, and a design to support the care of patients and to assist the medical staff in healing.

Designing an urban park in a low-income neighbourhood can have a transformative impact on local residents. Children need space to play outdoors. Kids need safe places to explore, hunt, get dirty, make up games, and interact with nature. Often, it is lower-income families who desperately need public spaces the most. We can't let our cities get sterile.

Greening buildings to reduce their carbon impact creates new standards for a sustainable community. Innovative housing, be it a small downtown condo or a new subdivision, offers the opportunity for an architect to reach beyond the standard and touch lives.

An architect can truly shape a city, as Antoni Gaudi has done with Barcelona and Georges-Eugène Haussmann did in Paris.

## Taking Action

If a community is going to seek, lead, and demand striking design, there are three fundamental elements that must be present.

First, the community must appreciate innovative design and understand how, through that design, it can be set apart from its competitors. There needs to be an intense commitment to make wonderful urban design a regular part of building a great city. Montreal has had a traditional commitment to interesting architecture and *protecting* its many historically-significant properties. Melbourne, on the other hand, has done a terrific job of *blending* renovated heritage buildings adjacent to modern high-rise buildings. Often, the transition is softened by appealing public spaces and striking public art.

Second, the council and the senior administration must have the courage to demand more of themselves and the private sector to raise the bar and elevate community design standards. They must understand the spatial importance of streets and open spaces, and how public buildings need to fit their surroundings. They must support the greening of public and private spaces. There must be an understanding of textures and materials in buildings; of interesting lighting on/in buildings; of why water features can add so much comfort to so many. Tough questions must be asked and answered. How much parking for cars? Will bicycles be accommodated? What are the links to the street frontage? How will the building blend into the neighbourhood? How will the community be elevated by the concept and usage?

Finally, there must be an acceptance that investing money in unique architecture, appealing design, and building wonderful public places and spaces is part of the economic and cultural development that will result in a more prosperous, competitive community. Vancouver has cleverly used private money from developers to enhance the public realm, and insisted on urban design that has resulted in attractive spaces that often include water features, urban landscaping, and interesting design elements. This blending of the public and private realm and creating "in between" places and spaces enhance any city's appeal and attractiveness, without breaking the public purse.

Governments have always played a role in how cities are designed and built. Whether it was a monarch during the Renaissance, a church leader's commitment to a great temple or cathedral, or elected representatives deciding to build a significant public place, government has always influenced design.

The private sector has usually been the one to execute, build, even finance projects, while the local government has been an arbiter, a provoker, and a demander of great projects. In more recent decades, however, those demands and lofty expectations have frequently disappeared behind a flurry of bureaucratic fumbling, political insensitivity to exciting new design opportunities, a fear of spending public dollars on iconic projects, and an unfocused community and council that collapses under scrutiny.

Jeff Fielding has been part of this debate for many years. He knows the realities. "Politicians don't understand the importance of good urban design. It is also difficult to regulate. Great design has to be market-driven and raise the bar in local communities. Developers can make money with interesting design, but you aren't often seeing the effort."

*Cities with buzz are attractive to creative people and investors; Hong Kong has built a colourful, robust downtown by building up, not out.*

The conflict between public and private is growing. There is frequently a disconnect between planners who are seen as petty rule enforcers, and developers who can be seen as running rough-shod over local regulations that are in place to protect a community, simply to save a few dollars and increase their profit margin.

What is very clear is that municipalities have not led strongly enough in demanding and expecting grand architecture – in public or private sector projects.

Our civic DNA is not as deeply entrenched with the demand and desire for epic architecture and memorable buildings as it is some cultures. According to Eddie Friel, part of this goes right back to the disposable North American society we have created.

"Over time, the issue of disposable goods also became disposable places," he argues. "It is almost as if anything more than 10 years old needs to be discarded. That kind of planned obsolescence of products and goods is something the 21st century mindset was educated to, and which has done serious damage to the quality of places.

"America is still a very young country. There is a different mindset from history in Europe – civilizations from Greek to Roman to Renaissance – that forms your culture, your identity; there's nothing you can do to discard that. If you're born into a culture that disposes of things, that has an impact on the way you're going to live. Very few municipal structures in North America are memorable."

Jack Diamond agrees. "It is that wise expenditure, that sense of the public realm, that we miss in life. The market doesn't regulate everything. It doesn't provide public space."

This is a crucial role for governments to play, particularly local governments, responsible for the shaping and design of their communities. How much of a focus they will put into urban design guidelines and demanding an elevated level of creativity and architectural innovation is a basic question that not enough councils confront.

In a candid interview with international planning expert Larry Beasley, we talked bluntly about urban design and the frequent failures of government to encourage innovation:

*GH: Great urban design has been missing from government projects for a long time ...*

**LB:** The people in control of these projects are not urban designers. Too often, we are applying standards and thinking that they've had for 30 years. It is more important [to them] to get vehicles around a new building than have a bunch of people hanging around the public space!

*GH: Who is in control of the process?*

**LB:** Urban designers, even if you can get them institutionalized in a government, are still advisors, not managers. We need to support greater consciousness of urban design. Dallas has [become aware] of the need to convert every aspect of the city to be more design-oriented and design-conscious. It is very hard to break into the managers who actually manage the change. They have all kinds of ways to keep you out. They have their standards, they talk of health and safety, security, liability ... all designed to keep the status quo.

*GH: How do we break through these barriers?*

**LB:** Money is a driver. A second driver, which is just as strong, is power. Who controls these places? If you can shift control to people who have the competencies, then you'll start to see changes that really work. Rotterdam is a good example – engineers work for the urban designer. People can start to make demands. Organize a group. Do a video of how terrible the street is. Social media. Do a big event.

*GH: People are ahead of politicians on this?*

**LB:** Right across the country, you find a very frustrated design community. In any city today, you find so much talent, so many ideas, and so much frustration.

*GH: How do municipal leaders move beyond?*

**LB:** We need to make politicians make it part of their platform. [e.g., former Chicago Mayor Daley pushing through Millennium Park]. Reorganize bureaucracies to make joint management imperative. Build alternative uses, design. We are starting to see engineers understand and act in some cities ... is the agenda of the public realm with planners or engineers?

*GH: Where is the leadership coming from?*

**LB:** [Communities] need a champion to force change. That could be a mayor, councillor, community rep, planner ... A lot of people are alienated, disempowered, from civic government. Municipalities need people, organizations, groups to show alternatives, bring forward ideas ... Municipalities should be educating the public on this. Philanthropists can lead and challenge old thinking ... advocate for it. [So can] community organizations and leaders.

This restlessness with the status quo, the seeking for change and new ways, is common throughout the interviews and research undertaken for this book. There is a strong feeling by many that the system is broken and we must do better.

There is also a sense that there is a serious disconnect between local government and the local community. The relationship has grown more distant; many feel the voice of the people isn't being listened to as much as it should be.

That may be a symptom of the growing demand for empowerment at the local level that has rippled through much of the world in recent years. Politicians are too often seen as isolated from the street and its realities. Bureaucrats are seen as impediments, not as enhancers and enablers of building wonderful modern communities. That reality may also be hampering truly original thinking and concepts from being shared by urban designers and architects.

Jack Diamond competes for government contracts, but too often finds that, with his firm's flair for design, the bureaucrats don't respect or give credit to innovation or creativity because they can't be quantified. He knows of bold urban concepts that have been rejected by committees of bureaucrats because design is so subjective. Therefore, in marking on a comparative basis, great design doesn't get points.

"Bureaucracy just fills in the blanks on the form ... the inspiration is absolutely missed. That's why we get grey concrete boxes built for governments. The system is set up for risk in the private sector ... in the public sector, there is no culture for that," he concludes.

The rules and regulations, and the constrictions and frustrations they place on innovation, reflect directly on the point made earlier by Jennifer Keesmaat: rules don't make sense if they aren't creating a great city. That is a point upon which everyone agrees. The challenge is changing the system.

## Money Talks

The second significant barrier to encouraging and supporting wonderful municipal urban design is money.

"Great municipal design/projects are difficult. [With the] infrastructure deficit, people are more concerned about the quality of pipes and roads than about urban design," acknowledges Jeff Fielding.

There is another purely political reason: politicians today don't want to be labeled as "wasting" taxpayers' money. As politicians will tell you, there will always be a negative voice in the community raised whenever any civic spending is proposed.

Efforts to get something approved – whether a new library branch or a sewage treatment plant – are bound to be met with hostility from someone or some group. Local media often focus on the negative, so those voices get lots of publicity. Politicians become so battered just from trying to get the project approved that they don't have the energy or passion to also fight for great design.

We've also seen a change in focus. "The really great public places of the last century were the railroad stations," says Jack Diamond. "These were a kind of public palace for the people to use."

He makes a very interesting observation on public spending and building: "There's been a shift. In Europe, it used to be that you had public grandeur and private squalor. In North America, we have private grandeur and public squalor – the exact opposite. It's what the last Pope called excessive capitalism. Taken to extremes, it is greed and selfishness. Everybody wants to be individualistic, which leads to the dearth of public space because they are doing it for themselves. Politicians are scared to invest in public places and spaces."

This even extends to the maintenance of public facilities. Politicians don't want to be seen spending on themselves, even though they would be protecting a public investment.

In Canada, perhaps the most egregious example is the reluctance of the Harper government to upgrade and repair 24 Sussex Drive – the historic home of our Prime Minister. The house is deteriorating and the cost to repair is likely $10M+. In a time of government constraint and hesitation to spend public money, the politicians in charge simply won't invest in protecting and preserving this public site.

This attitude impacts the maintenance of many government-owned facilities. It almost always results in a much larger bill at some point. As homeowners know, you've got to invest in maintenance of your house or the bill later will be enormous.

John Nicholson understands those political realities. "Politicians are driven by an attitude that if you spend, you are being a spend-thrift. Some won't see beyond that. [We can achieve] a reasonable development for public benefit. Not every public building needs to be a gateway building, a Shangri-La ... "

He offers the following interesting examples of thoughtful Canadian urban design.

*Montreal's Old Waterfront* – The cobblestones and the history of the old port offer a unique heritage experience for visitors today, who can also enjoy a fabulous array of great local restaurants and bars.

*Toronto's Distillery District* – Just east of downtown, this project restored the 1832 distillery into a hot urban pedestrian village, featuring cutting-edge culture, shopping, and entertainment.

*Vancouver's Granville Market* – This former industrial site went into dramatic decline and was not resurrected until the 1970s and 1980s. Today, it is a thriving eco-friendly island community, featuring a farmers' market, entertainment, and restaurants, and offering an exciting cultural vibe for residents and visitors.

While each project is unique, there are some important common elements:

➤ respect for heritage properties;

➤ pedestrian oriented, not vehicular;

➤ supports local culture, arts, artisans;

➤ focuses on local food, restaurants, entertainment, social environment, and meeting places; and

➤ creates a great experience for the visitor.

Some find it discouraging that money drives design, but that is the reality for municipalities and the other orders of government today.

And yet, there is still the other reality – cities need to differentiate themselves from their competitors. If every place starts to look the same, as some argue is typical of suburbs and gateways to cities today, lined with fast-food restaurants and mini-malls, how can a city be perceived as offering something special and unique?

The answer is often exciting, contemporary urban design. Creating a vibrant downtown. Offering interesting housing options. Preserving heritage properties. Building attractive public places. Animating provocative public spaces. Offering comfortable, safe, tree-lined streets.

As Professor Friel observes about the money versus design battle, "It is not either/or. A sense of place, quality of place must be identified. [Municipalities must] persuade [their public of the] need to invest in infrastructure. Cities need to generate wealth. Public policy should be based on how it will generate wealth. Investment in public places and spaces can help to attract people and generate wealth."

## Towns and Cities with Buzz

The judgment of a town or city starts the moment a visitor, potential investor, or someone looking to locate for a career first approaches that community. First impressions are difficult to change, and impressions start even before the arrival.

What does the municipality's website present? Is it up to date, easy to navigate, providing key information? Do the pretty pictures live up to actual scrutiny? What are the gateways like? When people fly or drive into the community, what are their impressions? Is the downtown clean and active? Do locals send out a great vibe? What's the social buzz in town? How are civic officials treating people?

Visitors understand the public library is both a safe place and a source of important information. Business people check out the street action, the retail activity, the hustle of a city. They want to be treated with respect and courtesy at city hall and by all government resources. A guy tossing the garbage on the truck can create just as important an impression as the ward councillor.

People naturally gravitate to public places and spaces. There is a physical response to a city. People look up at the towers. They walk down the main street. They sit on a patio and watch passers-by and feel the vibe. This response to the physical domain, the public places and spaces, and the intersection of the private and the public realm is a reflection of the city's personality. It is what people will talk about on social media or with friends.

People are attracted to beauty. Architecture and design are the foundation of a distinctive urban environment, suburban community, town, or village. Public buildings are a critical part of any community.

From parks to libraries, from city hall to museums, from the underground pipes that people never see to the great towers that they admire, public places and spaces make up so much of the impression, character, and reputation of a community. The civic DNA.

A community can be changed by a single council decision about what to build, where to build it, and how to design it. And, in Canada, of course, that often starts with a hockey rink.

# CHAPTER 5

# IF YOU DON'T BUILD IT, THEY WON'T COME

*"Leaders can inspire cities, and cities can inspire leaders." – Jim Hunt*

Municipal political leaders are faced with a blunt reality at some point in their efforts to push their communities into hosting great sports, entertainment, and tourism events: If you don't have the right venue, you're not going to attract the big events. If you don't have the big events, you won't attract the visitors and their economic benefits. If you don't have the venue and the events, you won't get the national and international exposure that so many cities crave.

In other words, if you don't build it, they won't come.

The cost of civic ownership or participation in paying some or all of the costs of these venues continues to rise, perhaps led by the glorious excesses of the $1.2B (USD) AT&T Stadium in Arlington, Texas where the Dallas Cowboys play. As the *Fort Worth Star-Telegram* noted, "As part of its contract, Arlington gets five percent of the annual naming-rights payments, not to exceed $500,000 a year ... the city should expect to receive the maximum, meaning that the deal is worth at least $10M a year. In 2004, Arlington voters approved a 30-year, $325M bond package to help build the stadium. Those bonds are being repaid with a half-cent sales tax, a two percent hotel occupancy tax, and a five percent car rental tax."

In contrast, voters in Katy, Texas in 2013 defeated a bond request to build a new 14,000-seat football stadium costing $70M – for their high school.

The Olympic Games are awarded to a city, not a country, but they have become financially impossible for cities. It is inconceivable today that federal and provincial governments would not make significant financial contributions for infrastructure and the enormous expense of security.

Costs have skyrocketed for bidding, building, and running major international sports events. The most costly Olympics in history were the 2014 Winter Olympics in Sochi, Russia: $51B.

Why do it? The answers are complex.

It's often about the legacy. Having the eyes of the world focused on your city. International media coverage. Attracting future investment. Travel and tourism opportunities. Building facilities and venues that can last for decades and benefit local residents, and perhaps become a national training centre. New affordable housing. Restoring a lost neighbourhood. Stunning new architectural designs for venues. Major international games can become the platform upon which to build other international or national bids, because that event will leave your city a place in history.

The Vancouver Winter Olympics in 2010 were a great example of intangible benefits as well. Large, peaceful crowds roamed the streets at night, having fun and celebrating. Tourists were embraced and locals unhesitatingly offered help to lost or bewildered visitors.

Canada also celebrated. The nation came together, riveted as Sydney Crosby scored the "Golden Goal" against the U.S. The host city and its partners were applauded, and the organizing committee, staff, and volunteers – who came from across Canada at their own expense – quite properly were recognized for running a great event.

Vancouver overcame challenges by Mother Nature and other incidents to become a success – and broke even financially.

London, England used the 2012 Summer Olympics and Paralympics as a catalyst for the rejuvenation of a large chunk of the city that was derelict. The sprawling east-end London site, renamed Queen Elizabeth Olympic Park, is now home to 2,800 families. The original budget was four billion pounds; the final cost was about nine billion.

## Community Ego or Community Benefit?

Making the decision to invest millions of public dollars in a multi-purpose arena/entertainment complex, stadium, or performing arts centre is usually one of the most controversial decisions that a municipal council will face.

While no one suggests that such a facility will solve all the local economic problems or transform a community, it can be an important catalyst as part of a larger civic strategy. It may attract new high-rise condo towers downtown, or new college/university faculties. More feet on the street generates more action, more bars and restaurants starting up, and perhaps occupancy for closed buildings or heritage properties.

Veteran international venue expert Brian Ohl believes a big part of the answer is community pride. "This can be something the residents point to that makes their community special. It adds to the quality of life. And, the development of areas in the community, often in the downtown core, can be a catalyst [for economic growth and prosperity]."

The most common facilities for communities of all sizes are sports/entertainment complexes (i.e., hockey/skating rinks that can be converted for use as entertainment venues for touring shows, conferences and trade shows, or big local events). In small and mid-sized communities, these venues often are part of a civic complex and may include a library, community meeting rooms, or fitness/health facility.

Generally, they don't make money. A community invests in these venues to improve its quality of life, support economic development, attract tourism dollars, enhance community pride, and spark new life in a moribund downtown or area around the new facility.

"In the Ontario Hockey League, only two venues [of 20 cities] make money," notes Brian Ohl. "The others are subsidized by the community. Even some NHL venues don't make money. They aren't profit-making ventures, so every community has to decide if benefits like community enhancement, pride of ownership, and economic opportunities are reasons to move ahead."

Having a great sports/entertainment complex provides distinctive opportunities to host big events. It also can have a substantial impact on what people think about that city, which may result in some interesting opportunities.

Olympic gold medalist Tessa Virtue has competed and performed in wonderful venues and great cities around the world. "I'm a city person. I find cities invigorating. I'm fascinated by how each has its own distinctive energy and vibe."

That energy is translated by the people. Asked about what elements she notices most in cities, her answer is instructive for municipal leaders: "I think the buzz of people. The style. I love fashion and seeing the different styles in Europe and Japan. Each city has its own colour ... the colours can really set the scene. I feel it physically when I'm walking around a city. There is a sense of overwhelming energy about it, and it is contagious."

Creating that buzz, that energy, and trending on social media is what smart, creative cities want. It gives them a competitive edge in attracting investment dollars and in the global hunt for talent. It supports a local climate of entrepreneurship, innovation, and creativity.

Conversely, without that buzz, cities gain a quite different reputation. "Harbin, China. I remember longing for home and the comfort of the known. There wasn't that level of sophistication or culture in the city. It was discouraging," Tessa Virtue says candidly. How did she see the colours of Harbin? "Grey. Very grey."

Does that affect performance? "I think so. The overall downcast feeling, especially in a place like Harbin ... When I'm performing in cities that I love, it is easier – you want to move, you want to perform, you want to expend that energy. It can be really draining when you're in a city that doesn't have that vibe."

In other words, cities need to develop a personality.

## Civic Decision Making

*Note: I was new on London city council in 1997 when a group of just-elected councillors became determined to invest in and improve the downtown core, which had fallen into a steep decline. We ended up investing about $100M in three main projects: the John Labatt Centre or JLC (renamed Budweiser Gardens in 2012 for a $6M fee), a new Central Library, and the Covent Garden Market (CGM). I was a strong proponent of all three, and make that full disclosure.*

How civic leaders build, design, and lead their communities has many ripples and repercussions. The decisions council members make will be scrutinized and evaluated for years.

London, Ontario made a major investment in three public facilities in the late 1990s to kick-start a depressed and depressing downtown core. The case study for these investments is detailed at the end of this chapter and explores the process, problems, and outcomes. A second case study then provides a briefer look at three other major sports/entertainment complexes proposed for Edmonton, Markham, and Quebec City. There are lessons for municipal leaders in all of them.

For London, those public investments were a catalyst for private sector investment. The downtown today is stronger and more vibrant than it was a dozen years ago. Assessment has grown 59 percent. Thousands more people – generally young professionals or retired empty-nesters – live downtown in well-appointed new highrise condos and apartment buildings. Western University and Fanshawe College have made significant commitments to new downtown campuses, bringing more students with their energy and enthusiasm to the core.

Locating the venue is a crucial decision, and the choice is downtown or in the suburbs. "I love when venues are in the downtown," says Tessa Virtue. "You feel you're in the city. I love the idea that someone can come watch us skate and then walk across the street and get a good dinner or go for a drink. Public places and spaces are hugely reflective of that community. It represents the city, the culture, the society – for good or for bad."

In London, you can barely get a downtown dinner reservation when the Knights hockey team plays. A sell-out crowd of 9,000+/game is virtually assured. It has become a major social event in London. As Brian Ohl says, "Budweiser Gardens helped to change the perception of London. People now recognize London as a vibrant market for hockey, the music scene, figure skating, and more. People want to be emotionally invested in what goes on at Bud Gardens and feel that sense of pride and ownership."

There is still work to be done in London's downtown – too many vacant stores and offices, not green enough, traffic patterns are awkward, sidewalks are a problem, there isn't enough action on the streets at noon hour and after work, no food trucks, and even more people living in the core are needed – but, without question, downtown London is better off today than many other North American cities.

Council learned that it had to step up, display confidence in the downtown's future, and invest first; the private sector investments followed.

## Lessons Learned

***Size matters*** – Budweiser Gardens is often sold out. London has earned a reputation as a great host for sports and music events, and that has become a focus of the city's tourism and marketing efforts. If you build it too small, you won't get the larger touring shows and major sporting events; if it is too large, empty seats create a discouraging, depressing environment.

***Back of house*** – As shows get bigger and more technically complex (it is not unusual for a large touring show to have 15 semi-trailers of staging and equipment), and sports events demand more TV and media space, you will need more room back of house. That can be accomplished with an expansion of non-public locations, but will come at a cost. It is important to allow as much flexibility in the design as possible. Technology demands will simply grow.

*Public patio/square* – In London, council was so focused on the building design and details that it didn't think much about the public space around the building. As a result, the external square is concrete, poorly designed, and not particularly user-friendly. Changes in recent years have added a water feature and some public art, and the street adjacent can be closed to make a larger public square when linked with the Covent Garden Market piazza. The council of the day, including me, should have done a better job.

*Do it right* – If you're going to go to the trouble and expense of building major facilities, don't cheap out at the end trying to save a few dollars. Investments in quality are almost always the right choice. London's council held firm on that practice, and it has paid off for the city.

## Decision Points

*Public support/demand* – There will be controversy. There will be negativity. There will be opposition. Are you and your council colleagues prepared for the battle? Is it winnable? Can you stand up to the public scrutiny and media pressures? Is council committed?

*Research* – Think through the entire project and its ramifications. Is your market/community big enough to support it? What will be the impact on existing sports, arts, cultural, and community organizations and venues? How will it impact other economic development opportunities? Where is the private sector?

*Consultants* – Outside experienced eyes can be useful. But, they are only consultants; they are not infallible; and, at the end of the day, YOU will be held accountable and responsible for the final decision and the success or otherwise of the project. Nobody will remember the name of the consultant.

*Media relations* – There will be intense media interest and speculation. How are you going to handle media questions? One spokesperson? Political games? Leaks? Media polling that may or may not support your position? Such a project will cross many traditional community borders and draw in a wider range of commentators and opponents than usual. It will be a front-page story, not a sports story.

*Location* – This is a huge decision point. Are you going downtown
or suburban? Does the municipality control the land or will you
have to buy it? If word leaks out, how do you stop landowners from
seeking windfall profits? What impact will the new venue have on
businesses and potential businesses around the site?

*Catalyst* – Can it spur private sector development? Can it encourage new housing? Can it be a multi-purpose public facility (e.g., a
restaurant/bar open to the public, regardless of whether an event is
inside)?

*Major tenants* – Who will be your major tenant? How many nights
a year will the facility be booked? *(London originally budgeted for
85 to 90 nights a year ... Bud Gardens has delivered twice that.)*
What is your growth potential?

*Who will run it?* – The municipal council shouldn't be involved in
management and operating decisions. Do you really want council
debating the price of popcorn or a cup of beer? Hire professional
managers. Give them authority. Hold them accountable.

*Design is important* – You want an architecturally-significant building – it will be there for the next half-century. Think through the
internal needs, get professional advice, bring your common sense,
and ask questions. And, don't forget about the opportunities for innovative design *outside* the venue, which should create an exciting
new public space.

*Nail the business plan* – You've got capital costs. You've got operating costs. You need a capital fund to finance repairs and upgrades.
Will you make a profit? Likely not. Is the community prepared to
subsidize ongoing operating losses to gain the other benefits the
venue will provide? What policies should you implement to encourage community access, which usually rents at a much lower rate?

*Have courage* – This kind of project – and the decision – will often
be the biggest issue that council members will consider during
a term of office. It will not generate unanimous public approval.
Council will be divided. This is a hard, tough process. If you're not
prepared for the battle, don't start the war.

*The John Labatt Centre in London, Ontario (now Budweiser Gardens) helped to spark a downtown rejuvenation for this mid-sized city. Photo: Baden Roth*

Brian Ohl offers an insider's view on why some projects are more successful than others. "Location. Population. Market. Local media. Right spot – the location has to make sense for that community. It is often easier and offers more benefits if it is downtown. Good management. A great main tenant – one that is successful, supportive, wants to win; there must be a local ownership/commitment, and be seen as part of community."

He adds, "Venues have to be flexible (especially in smaller markets). [For touring shows] it can't be a hassle to get in or get set up. There are a lot more markets than good touring acts. The [entertainment] industry is tight-knit ... word gets around within a week of problems with a venue or its management or market."

Tessa Virtue has smart advice for municipalities about the importance of little details. "We're lucky that our venues are a controlled space ... but physically, venues can vary. For example, the areas where we warm up, maybe where the ice machine comes off, is it dirty, puddles on the ground where we're trying to stretch? We like to find our own space. That becomes our little home away from

home, where we go through our routines. Sometimes, if there isn't
the space, you're warming up right beside your competitors. That
can be mentally challenging.

"On the ice, colour is a big thing. We have so much white ice, and
with the TV lights, everything is bright and there is not that feeling of intimacy with the crowd if everything is white. I like when
there's colour in the stands – the seats or billboards. If there's a lot
of natural light coming, it can be great, but can be blinding. Sometimes, the rinks are quite barren. The stands are set up so far from
the rink that you don't get the sense that you're really performing
for the audience – you're an afterthought. At Budweiser Gardens,
the venue is intimate – the crowd is right there. You can reach over
and grab some popcorn! With a crowd being close, it just adds to the
level of performance."

She concludes with a simple but powerful statement: "Everything
matters – whether it is a smile from a volunteer before you take the
ice or just the familiarity of colours, everything matters. Performers
all have their favourite venues. Whether it is the catering, whatever.
The quality of the local venue is a huge deciding factor for events.
Size, location, volunteers, everything that makes an event run."

These are the fine details that municipal leaders need to know and
understand. Talk to building operators, visit other markets and
venues to find out what worked – and what didn't. And, when
you're visiting, talk to the guys building the stage, not just the GMs.

## Hosting Big Events

One of greatest benefits to building a wonderful new venue for
sports and entertainment is that the door begins to open to host
internationally-renowned entertainers, national and even world
championships – and those events can help to change a city's image.

What can these opportunities do for a city? Brian Ohl says, "You
see activity, people, noise, energy of people on the streets. You can
feel it the day of a big concert. They provide vibrancy, add energy
to the community. Playoff series get people talking about the game.
People talk about how great the show was. You feel good about your
community – and people spend money."

Yes, they do. The 2013 World Figure Skating Championships' "total economic activity brought an estimated benefit to London of $32.1M. The Memorial Cup projected total economic activity of $10M," according to London Tourism GM John Winston. Sports tourism has now become a central part of the city's tourism and economic strategies.

There are many community benefits as well, says Tessa Virtue. "It is a very important investment. It can bring people together ... that's something I've learned through sports. Be it the Olympics or an OHL hockey game or a concert, those are the things that unite people and transport people and allow people to step away from reality for a few moments or a few hours, and that's what many people live for. It is a hugely important thing."

How do communities, especially smaller cities, compete with much larger cities that have hosted the same events? Interestingly, sports organizations and entertainment moguls are learning that smaller communities sometimes offer the best value, and they will "own" the community for that moment. They aren't paying big-city prices for hotels, media, venues, and hospitality. They aren't lost in the media shuffle of a metropolitan area.

Brian Ohl offers great advice: "Getting national/international events starts years in advance. The local market needs to host regional, national events. Treat them well ... skaters need to like the ice ... local media supportive ... the municipality needs to get behind the event. Then, you work with national organizations, find partnerships, and develop a reputation for hosting great events.

"There is a shift in markets – organizations are now seeking mid-sized cities, rather than just the largest metro markets. Yet, organizations need to make money on their championship or event ... so it has to be a certain size, there may need to be financial guarantees," he adds.

That is why a city like London, Ontario can compete on the world stage with Moscow, Los Angeles, Paris, Tokyo, and the other hosts of the World Figure Skating Championships.

## Big, BIGGER, **BIGGEST!**

Jaws have dropped at the money being spent on international sporting events and their venues. The 2014 World Cup in Brazil and the Rio Summer Olympics in 2016 have combined for capital investments approaching $50B, and the meter is still running.

Some of the investment for such events is for infrastructure that would be spent regardless – things like a light rail system extending to an airport, or the athlete's village that can be converted to affordable housing for local residents.

Disappointingly, however, wonderful venues often fall into disuse and disrepair after the major event for which they were built. I had a private tour of the Bird's Nest stadium in Beijing at the start of their Olympic Games. It was an innovatively-designed structure with its own beauty. Today, people who have recently been in Beijing report that it is barely used and is deteriorating. Sad.

Similarly, the future use of Sochi's venues is very much in question.

In fact, facilities in many Olympic host cities are often abandoned. The volume of tourists and important sports events quickly dry up. The municipality can't afford the upkeep on these large venues, and they rapidly slide into disrepair. It seems such a waste to spend hundreds of millions on a facility for a two-week event, and then see the community abdicate its support.

A University of Oxford study of 17 Olympics concluded that there was a 100 percent chance of the Games exceeding their budgets; the average cost overrun was 179 percent. Other studies have shown that the predicted economic benefits have often not accrued or lasted in Olympic cities.

New business models are needed. Fresh thinking is required on the design, location, and construction of capital projects to ensure a life-after. The best indicator of future success and usage seems to be established local need and support for a facility, or a plan for how a venue can be adapted for specific local purposes.

The cost of bidding for major international events is high. One has to hope that some sanity will return to the process. Mid-sized cities risk being cut out, even though they could undoubtedly host a great championship. There has to be a correction. The costs are simply getting out of reach.

******

The following case studies offer a detailed look at four significant Canadian municipal investments – one with a 10-year track record, and three others in various stages of development. For comparison purposes, they are all "sports/entertainment" facilities; but, the concepts and decision points could equally refer to a proposed performing arts centre, new city hall, or other major public facility. These studies show the complexities and challenges faced by a council when it considers such major capital expenditures, and lessons from which other communities can learn.

## Case Study #1: Downtown revitalization, London, Ontario

### Scenario

➤ Downtown London had sunk into a typical scenario for North American cities in the 1980s and 1990s: Suburban malls had sucked retail traffic from the core. Long-time retailers had fled or closed. The promises of a downtown retail mall that had been built in the 1980s (ill-designed with solid brick walls that closed off the mall to the public) soon failed. It destroyed many retail businesses surrounding the mall, and changed pedestrian traffic patterns. Downtown was increasingly perceived as dirty, dangerous, and unappealing. Few people lived downtown, and you could shoot cannons down the streets on a frigid January evening.

➤ London's "Ice House" was an old, small, cramped, and ugly building on the outskirts of the city, just off the highway. It seated 5,000, but the city's major junior hockey team, the London Knights, had never won a championship and weren't filling that building.

➤ The Covent Garden Market, in downtown London since 1845 with a couple of different iterations, was crumbling. Literally. Decades of slush and salt had eroded the steel and concrete parking lot that was above the market vendors. The market was loved by locals, but they were less keen about chunks of it falling on their heads.

➤ Attempts over the years to have the city build a new performing arts centre had all met with failure. The 1967 Centennial Hall was a poorly-designed multi-use facility that had undergone decades of band-aids and patchwork efforts to improve the sound quality, patron comforts, and staging facilities; but, as the old saying goes, "you can't put lipstick on a pig."

➤ London's municipal councils had a reputation of not investing in the city. Or, when they did, too often doing it on the cheap (see Centennial Hall, above).

➤ It was in that environment that half of London's council members elected in 1997 were brand new, and vigorously determined to make change, rejuvenate the downtown, and quite frankly kick London in its butt to get things moving again. They genuinely didn't care about the political consequences; the new brooms quickly grabbed hold of the council agenda.

## Action

➤ Council created a Millennium Task Force. Surprisingly, 11 of the 19 members chose to sit on it, most of them the newly elected members. This meant whatever the committee decided was pretty much assured of council support. Ten major projects were identified, including a couple of important but lesser magnitude actions, such as improving street lighting and better street/sidewalk cleaning.

➤ Community and political debate began immediately. It quickly became clear that the market project, which had been discussed by the previous council, had to proceed. The old building was torn down and a new building constructed on that site.

➤ The venerable old Central Library desperately needed a new, larger facility with modern technology. The concept of purchasing the closed Bay Store in the downtown mall was innovative *(again, full disclosure: I was chair of the library board and it was my idea)*. Council funded the $25M renovation. An extensive public fundraising campaign raised $6M to enhance the library. The community was very supportive.

➤ The major project became the proposed sports and entertainment complex. Four sites were identified, including both downtown and highway locations. Public opinion was split. There were people for, people against. Some loudly: Too expensive. City won't support it. Wrong location. No parking. Disrupts downtown traffic patterns. Debt. Woe to all.

➤ A dirty, vacant parking lot downtown was finally purchased by the city for $10M. On that site, many years before, had been a thriving city block, hotel, and music club – but it was now a rat-infested, pigeon-pooping, crumbling wreck. Despite that reality, a bunch of Londoners held hands around the block to save it.

➤ Once the city had acquired the site, it looked for consultants, partners, and architects. The design was to replicate the streetscape's heritage features. The council was smart enough to realize it couldn't run this process. A strong administrative team was formed to guide council, and did an outstanding job.

➤ The consultants recommended a cautious 6,500 seats. Council rejected that in a critical, hard-fought decision, and agreed on nearly 10,000 seats. There were public protestations and fears about the lack of parking, traffic patterns, the cost, and questions about whether the city would ever fill it. Council – or, more accurately, a majority of the council of the day – stood firm.

➤ A unique public/private partnership was developed that was believed to be a first in the industry. The managing company would be Global Spectrum from Philadelphia, an experienced company that managed many other properties in the U.S., owned major sports teams, and was prepared to be an investor. They became the facility manager. Council would not be involved in day-to-day operations. EllisDon, a major locally-based construction company, was the second private sector partner. They built the building.

## Financial

➤ The capital contributions were approximately:

- City of London          land purchase          $10 million
- City of London          capital contribution     34 million

- Private sector partners    capital contribution    10 million
- Canada + Ontario                SuperBuild Fund      5 million

                      Total capital cost             $59 million

- Interest payments                                                  $22 million

➤ Operating and profit-sharing:

- Years 1-5        City/private partners: 20/80%
- Years 6-10      City/private partners: 45/55%
- Years 11+       City/private partners: 70/30%

The deal was designed to let the private sector partners get their
money at the front end, and the city to enjoy the long-term benefits
and dividends.

## Outcomes

➤ The new Covent Garden Market opened in October 1999. Today, there is a waiting list for tenants, a number of lively community festivals are held on the public square, an outdoor farmers' market operates part of the year, and a skating rink attracts
people in the winter.

➤ In August 2002, the new Central Library was officially opened.
That building gave a great new anchor to the downtown in the
east end, with the JLC and CGM in the west. More than one
million people a year visit the downtown branch. Some would
argue it saved the mall that surrounds it, which was on the verge
of bankruptcy. The library includes a 400-seat theatre that is
booked most nights of the year, is the host to the London Arts
Council and the Heritage Council, as well as other community organizations, and provides several heavily-used meeting
rooms. The converted space (previously a department store) has
been studied by other librarians and urban designers as a great
example of re-purposing and re-designing a facility.

➤ The John Labatt Centre (now Budweiser Gardens) opened in
October 2002. Cher was the first act. Since then, a wide variety
of international superstars, from Elton John to Shania Twain,
have appeared. The London Knights have grown to be among
the most successful major junior hockey organizations in Can-

ada, having played in consecutive Memorial Cup tournaments in 2012, 2013, and 2014 – a rare feat.

➤ The Knights won the Memorial Cup for the first time in franchise history in 2005 – at the JLC in London, before a rabid crowd of supporters and an enthralled national TV audience watching Sydney Crosby play his last junior hockey game. It is interesting to speculate whether the Knights would have had that same success without their new home rink.

➤ The JLC has paid a dividend to its owners every year. Yes, it makes money. The building has hosted major national and international events, including the 2013 World Figure Skating Championships, the World Synchronized Skating Championships, two Memorial Cups, the Brier, and the Tournament of Hearts. More recently, it also became home to the two-time champions of the National Basketball League of Canada, the London Lightning. Even Londoners who strongly opposed the project today admit that they can't imagine downtown London without the facility, which is now the third-most successful venue for its size in the world, as determined by an international association.

Independent analysis since those public investments has shown the private sector has invested over $400 million in downtown London, with dramatic increases in the number of people living in the core. There was also a certain civic momentum created, which for several years helped London push ahead.

## Case Study #2: Edmonton, AB – Quebec City, QC – and Markham, ON

*Note: These community situations were somewhat fluid when this was written; subsequent events may have changed costs and even the project after the book went to print.*

### Quebec City

➤ Ground has been broken on the new "multi-purpose amphitheatre" near the downtown in Quebec City. The project will cost $400M, split between the provincial and municipal government.

There is a small private sector contribution for naming rights and management fees.

➤ Municipal dollars will come from borrowing and from a surcharge on tickets.

➤ The city is hoping to again attract an NHL hockey team. The Nordiques, playing in the NHL's smallest market, had serious financial problems in the 1990s and subsequently were sold and departed in 1995 for Denver. Ironically, the new team, renamed the Colorado Avalanche, won the Stanley Cup the next year.

➤ There is no guarantee of an NHL team re-locating to Quebec City, or (even more improbably in the near future) a new franchise being awarded to the city. The new Colisée (also known as the Quebecor Arena) is scheduled to open in 2015 and will be used for music and entertainment events, as well as sports.

➤ The proponents of the new facility have indicated they are looking long term to attract an NHL team. Many of the same issues that drove the former team out – primarily a small, uni-lingual French market – remain.

## Edmonton

➤ A new $600M complex is planned in downtown Edmonton. The city is home to the Edmonton Oilers, a successful NHL team for many years, although the franchise has not made the playoffs recently. The Wayne Gretzky era remains a fond highlight of the local sports scene.

➤ Funding for the new project will come from several sources, both public and private.

➤ Municipal funding will come from different streams:

• $140M from the city through taxes and a community revitalization levy; and

• $125M from a ticket tax, proceeds of which will be used to pay down the capital loan and interest.

➤ Private sector funding will include $115M from the owner of the Oilers, as part of the lease arrangement.

➤ Other funding is to come from a combination of private sector and other government financing.

➤ The city expects the new facility to spark rejuvenation of an under-developed neighbourhood, creating new tax revenue and development opportunities. It will expand seating from the current rink, increase revenue opportunities for the hockey club, as well as providing a new venue for concerts and other events.

## Markham

➤ One of the fastest-growing cities in Canada, Markham is located immediately north of Toronto. While the idea of a municipality of 300,000 building a 20,000-seat arena may seem incongruous, the reality is that growth of communities around Toronto has exploded. The arena was intended to draw from a population of five million in the GTA.

➤ The proposed project was part of a larger concept to develop a sports complex, university campus, performing arts centre, high-density housing, and other elements, including office space and a hotel and retail component.

➤ The entire project was estimated to cost $725M. The arena would cost $325M, the rest of the development $400M.

➤ The original proposal was a complex financing strategy: the town would borrow the $325M for the arena from a private sector partner, which would pay back half of that loan. The city would finance the other half through a surcharge on tickets, parking revenue, and a levy paid by developers when they built new houses. After resistance from some taxpayers, a new deal was proposed: the private sector partners would assume the entire construction cost, with $120M to come from housing developers who could eventually recoup some costs. The city would own the new rink, but it would be privately managed.

➤ Financing for the other part of the development would come from the municipality, with much of those costs for street and highway redevelopment, parking, and downtown improvements.

➤ Obviously, the ultimate hope is to attract a new or transferred NHL team. That is problematic, because the territorial rights are held by the Toronto Maple Leafs. As Hamilton and its Copps Coliseum found out, territorial rights are sacrosanct for professional sports owners. (The NHL dislikes communities that try to beat the drums over the relocation of an existing team, or lobby for a new franchise. Winnipeg was exemplary in regaining an NHL franchise with the move of the Atlanta team a couple of years ago. The city has embraced its Jets and the 15,000-seat MTS Centre that has sparked renewed activity downtown.) As a result, the Markham arena would have no main anchor tenant initially.

➤ Community reaction to this major development proposal has been sharply divided, as was council.

➤ After further controversy, Markham council voted in December 2013 to not provide public financial support for the project. Mayor Frank Scarpitti later admitted it would now "be tough" to attract an investment [for an NHL rink] of that size to Markham.

******

These case studies are fascinating examples of the differences in local cities and how they develop and finance large projects, how their municipal councils see opportunities, and how they envision the future and reach for it.

There are no hard and fast rules for a community's investments in public venues. What is certain is that municipalities are the ones driving such projects. There are lots of land mines that can blow up politically and financially, but also many substantive, long-term community benefits.

# CHAPTER 6

# NATIONS OF CITIES

*"What is the city but the people?"* – *William Shakespeare*

We are becoming nations of cities.

Many struggle with this new reality. Many politicians haven't yet understood that the global shift is increasingly towards cities and regions as the economic drivers, rather than nations. Smart students figured this out a while ago – they want a good job when they graduate, borders mean nothing to them, and they are choosing great cities (as opposed to countries) in which to live and work.

This is going to have a significant impact on the traditional "pecking order" of governments. Change, which never comes rapidly in government relations, is going to have to happen for many dominions. The traditional paternalistic relationship between various orders of government must change. Municipalities are on the rise.

Local governments need more taxing authority and sustainable revenue sources that are not based on the antiquated property tax system. Municipalities need more autonomy. And, they need an enhanced ability to develop their own international links and partnerships – which will impact traditional federal regulations on foreign investment, immigration, and trade. It may become a tumultuous time in intergovernmental relations in the years ahead, as municipalities assert their new, more dominant role.

Important new regional economic partnerships will mark the beginning of a new era of cooperation between municipalities, many of which may have had a history of regional competition and even combativeness for economic development. These cities and regions will realize that creating strong hubs for research, high-tech industries, and very modern manufacturing plants; attracting clusters of smart, creative thinkers; as well as offering an improved scale to keep business costs down and innovation up, are more important than lingering old high school football battles between former rivals.

While this in no way diminishes the enormous importance of rural and agricultural regions, or small towns and villages (and in fact offers the larger scenario where food production, entrepreneurship, and ensuring safe fresh water will become of even greater importance), the trend and the reality of urban life are inexorable.

Cities are now leading economic, social, cultural, business, living, and family development. We are entering a new era of municipal strength and prosperity for cities and regions that have the tools, vision, and opportunity to generate wealth and jobs, provide a great quality of life, and will commit to becoming leading global competitors. Most importantly, cities need strong leadership to accomplish these goals.

Cities drive national economies and international trade. Medical, scientific, and health care advances are often the result of new partnerships between and amongst key cities around the world, and the universities and hospitals in those cities. Advanced manufacturing agreements are emerging, linking far-flung cities and their industrial bases. Cultural enterprises from fashion design to movie production are global businesses that are based in key cities and that generate significant jobs and investment.

Cities are adapting and adopting new economic development priorities to take advantage of these glowing opportunities. Mayor-to-mayor agreements are augmenting, sometimes even replacing, the old federally-driven model, in which plane loads of politicians and bureaucrats arrived in some foreign country for a few days of a trade junket, replete with ceremonial signings but not always real economic results.

Increasingly, we are seeing direct city-to-city and region-to-region partnerships and alliances. A great example was the 2013 Global Cities Economic Partnership between Chicago and Mexico City, signed by the mayors of the two cities. That agreement focused on tourism, trade, innovation, and education.

This new kind of economic partnership, signed between two cities, often includes universities, hospitals and medical research facilities, environmental initiatives, business alliances, and cultural networks. They are an important new trend in alliances between municipalities, and offer economic and cultural benefits to both cities. They are done directly, without other orders of government, as the networks of cities and metro regions push their own economic strategies.

## A New Generation of Strong Local Leaders

Cities are starting to demand a voice in immigration placements, and are taking concrete action to make their communities more appealing to foreign investors, students, and workers. How these new residents are welcomed by the community, where and how they live, and the accessibility to familiar foods and places of worship are critical opportunities for progressive cities.

These are new and different roles for local government. This shift is also why building attractive, livable, and sustainable cities with a great quality of life is so vital to driving local prosperity.

The needs, focus, and opportunities are huge. Smart communities are changing. What usually hasn't changed is their relationship with other orders of government.

Municipalities struggle with inadequate resources to finance their development. They often operate in jurisdictions with inadequate governance authority, and too often are led by politicians who don't understand the emerging global business environment.

Municipal political leaders need to respect the demands of running billion-dollar corporations that are now competing in a global economy, while at the same time understanding that most of the jobs in their communities will come from the nurturing and growth of existing small and medium-sized businesses.

New alliances and powerful new voices can emerge when local government leaders partner with business and union leaders – for example, to advocate for more funding for infrastructure needs. Community and social advocates need to step forward and work with municipalities on shaping and supporting sustainable, safe, and healthy neighbourhoods.

At the same time, city halls need to have a hard look in the mirror. As these new, larger responsibilities emerge, we need a new breed of local leaders – tough, smart, creative, aware of the global challenges and opportunities, not content with the status quo, prepared to fight other orders of government to demand fundamental change in the traditional paternalistic relationship, and open to doing business differently. They must move the urban agenda forward.

They also need to understand the public realm; the places and spaces in their communities; the importance of the design of buildings and the provision of a leafy green oasis in the downtown core; and how young people can build equity in the costly housing market. These are all indicators of a 21st century city that can participate successfully in our global culture and economy.

Communities can't shrink their way to greatness.

## Changing How They Do Business

I asked a prominent private developer what was the one thing about city hall that he would change. The answer was succinct and blunt: "Attitude."

I asked a top Canadian planner what was the one thing about developers that he would change. That answer was also succinct and blunt: "Attitude."

The chasm between public and private sector interests has perhaps never been seen as so insurmountable as it is today. Paradoxically, with the severe limitations of the public purse, never has the need and opportunity for private sector involvement and public private partnerships (P3s) been so predominant. In 2013, P3s generated $51B for the Canadian economy.

Landowners and developers are frustrated by what they see as the never-ending merry-go-round of approvals, studies, political juggling, and ever-more staff tweaking. The private developer went on to comment, "City hall shouldn't make us feel second-class or that we're trying to promote some scam or something ... " It was a very sad commentary on the state of relationships between developers, builders, planners, and politicians.

Provincial and federal agencies and ministries seem to trip all over themselves with often confusing, even conflicting, rules, regulations, reviews, and demands for more research.

Municipal staff are expected to produce rapid approvals. Yet, they too are often constrained by existing by-laws and policies, provincial guidelines and policy statements, and even internal conflict over everything from stormwater management ponds to the design of neighbourhood streets.

Some municipalities have tried to expedite the approvals process by clarifying rules on applications, setting time periods for staff responses, and even forming consolidated departments by drawing several different areas from city hall together. The process has met with decidedly different results from community to community. A few municipalities have been successful, many have not, usually because of staff inertia or lack of political will.

Environmentalists are becoming more active in many municipalities, which too often inevitably sets up conflict with both city hall and the private sector. They should share common goals.

Architects are in the middle, frequently wanting to design innovative projects, but constrained by dollars and by developers arguing with municipal officials who lack a clear vision. As Larry Beasley says, the design community across Canada is frustrated.

The public looks on in dismay as the process lurches and farts. Public engagement is too often conducted in a bored and perfunctory manner that leaves all participants dissatisfied.

Politicians range from being ignored and on the periphery, to being dumped abruptly into a fire storm and being torn in many directions by lobbyists and staff. They are often unprepared or unwilling to make bold decisions.

Process often tops performance. Fierce deadlocks between partici-pants cause more delays, more public antipathy, more accusations and finger-pointing. Even definitions about zoning, planning, and by-laws can be argued.

It is a lousy, lousy process. On that, everyone can agree.

## A New Way of Thinking: Regional Planning

"Auckland had been the basket case of cities," admits Ludo Camp-bell-Reid. "It grew up in a very difficult time for cities and it went down the wrong path. It followed a path that LA took of cheap oil ... even some Canadian cities ... this is a story that has tracked around the world. Auckland is not alone, but it is alone in the exuberance with which it pursued that lifestyle."

The catalyst for change was 2007/2008, when the former prime minister wanted to build a rugby stadium on one of Auckland's wharfs. The eight mayors of the cities that made up the region at the time (it used to be 30) were invited to meet. They couldn't agree on a site. The cities had all been very selfish in their planning. It was their inability to come together that spurred the federal government (New Zealand has no state government) to appoint a Royal Com-mission to look into the governance of Auckland. It became a sem-inal moment in New Zealand's history when the government drove the unification through in 2010.

Today, the Auckland Plan is a bold, invigorating $9B, 30-year plan to replace the dreary, desolate, and dangerous parts of the city with the exciting genesis of a reborn community. It is trying to embed the plan with its philosophies and behaviours so deeply that future may-ors and councils can't derail the direction: $40M heritage fund; bold targets about sustainability and carbon emissions; aggressive targets for GDP; and over 100 urban planners and designers in city hall.

The difference is obvious – regional planning instead of small, paro-chial thinking. That is going to be one of the biggest shifts in plan-ning and servicing land in the years ahead. Cities need to get away from protectionist planning and constipated strategies to understand the new demands for regional thinking and economic development. That will demand broader planning objectives and greater strategic thinking about infrastructure investments, public transportation, environmental responsibilities, and the servicing of land.

The Capital Region Board (CRB) in northern Alberta was created in 2008 with representatives from 24 municipalities, including Edmonton. The mandate was to establish regional partnerships for growth, and to recognize the benefits of shared infrastructure, development, and policy frameworks. In other words, towns and cities are now looking at long-term planning decisions from a regional point of view. Municipalities that may be 50 kilometres away understand that decisions in one community affect the growth and development of others.

The CRB is focused on the integration of regional land use policies, inter-municipal transit, social and market affordable housing, and GIS, with an emphasis on infrastructure planning. How and where land will be serviced has vast implications on future growth and development. The regional approach offers local municipalities greater participation in that decision-making process, and provides greater certainty of long-range planning.

This larger vision of community planning is a clear model for the future. There are always great tensions amongst municipalities when a larger city starts clearing its throat and muttering about annexation. That process is almost always messy – even bloody. At the same time, small towns nibbling away just outside an urban growth boundary can provide highly sensitive tensions as well. Regional planning can help.

Public transportation routes don't end at a municipal border. The placement of sewers and roads determines residential and commercial growth. Nobody wants a new landfill site, but they have to go somewhere. Protecting good agricultural land from encroachment is a growing concern for many.

Looking at larger swaths of land for regional planning purposes is going to be a significant trend in the years ahead. Municipalities have to think outside their borders. Planning needs and developing

strong job and economic opportunities for their region will require
new strategic thinking from municipal leaders.

## Building a New Local Governance Structure

In most countries, federal governments provide very substantial
funding for urban growth and development, including networks of
high-speed rail, modern highways, urban infrastructure, and housing
support.

In mature democracies with developed economies (the United
States, some Commonwealth countries, some European nations, and
a few others), the federal government has not traditionally played
a substantial role in funding urban development. The ability and
authority of local governments to raise money is often severely restricted. Municipalities are clearly the third tier.

The traditional North American property tax system is broken and
can't be fixed, according to most municipal experts. It was simply
never intended to pay for all of the modern costs of building and
running a great city. Public transit is a tremendous issue; so is housing, downtown renewal, pipes, and pavement. As a result, the infrastructure deficits are climbing, even as every municipality's ability
to fund repairs, let alone growth, is falling behind.

Many cities that have been the traditional leaders in industry, job
creation, and innovation have been left behind. And, paralyzed by
fear, parochialism, and small thinking, federal, state, and provincial
politicians offer only tired rhetoric and useless platitudes, instead of
working with local governments to create vibrant new economies.

Many urban leaders have simply decided that they can't wait for
a slow, dysfunctional, and increasingly polarized congress, parliament, or legislature to take action. Many local leaders don't want
the fate of their community in the flailing hands of inept federal
politicians. They are too slow, too partisan, too out of touch, too
remote.

Many business and municipal leaders around the world looked on
in shock and horror as the U.S. Congress, with the federal government already shut down, rolled the dice with the global economy in

October 2013. Facing the unthinkable economic shock of defaulting and not being able to pay its bills, the largest economy in the world shuddered as its elected officials let partisan politics push the crisis to within hours of default.

At about the same time, in the throne speech in Canada opening a new parliament (similar to the state of the union address in the U.S., where the agenda for the country is laid out), the government seemed to be of the opinion that one of the most important issues facing Canadians was how they could purchase cable television channels.

Thinking people in both nations snorted and turned away; approval ratings for federal politicians plummeted even further. There was no recognition from these federal governments that a new era is emerging. Communities need help to develop their full potential.

From Asia to the Americas, from Africa to Australia, urban life is taking over. Cities are rising in global importance, and city-to-city partnerships will become as important as traditional nation-to-nation trade treaties.

It only seems reasonable to create a fairer division of consumption taxes (such as income, gas, and sales taxes) with Canadian municipalities. This will demand provincial governments stepping forward, as Saskatchewan did in 2011 when it began to share one of the five percent PST with its towns and cities. It is a Canadian first, and should be applauded.

New revenue streams for municipalities such as congestion charges, highway tolls, steeper downtown parking rates, development charges that fully reflect local costs, vehicle registration, local property transfer taxes, and other "user pay" fees are likely to be implemented in the future. Municipalities are desperate for non-property tax based revenue.

It also means municipalities must emerge with a clearer definition of their authority and ability to govern in the 21st century. The old attitudes from federal, provincial, or state elected officials and bureaucrats must change. Local governments need a stronger, more modern governance model. They must have clear authority in their areas of control, and then find the courage to use that new authority. We must reduce and eliminate duplication and waste between the orders of government.

Canada's provinces have to get over their arrogance about their power and their fear of loosening the chains on local governments; otherwise, they risk becoming increasingly impotent and irrelevant. Cities will pass them because economic, cultural, and social realities will eventually win.

The smart jurisdictions are the ones who see this new trend emerging and who take proactive steps now to recognize the changing roles and to support new economic trends.

State, provincial, and federal governments in nations with developed economies need to be thinking now about this new relationship with municipalities. At the same time, local governments need to be growing their own capacity for larger thinking, stronger leadership, greater vision, and more accountability.

## Building the Intellectual Capacity

Traditionally, progressive communities have recognized that they need to both *attract* and *retain* bright minds, entrepreneurs, innovators, and job-creators. In a word, their human capital.

Today, we need to add an additional component to the mix: those assets must also be *developed.*

Once a community attracts these clusters of bright minds, once you can retain them, then communities need to support, encourage, and be a catalyst for developing and enhancing this intellectual capacity.

Cities are uniquely positioned to gather creative, innovative thinkers – who in turn support a local climate focused on innovation and ideas, and turning those ideas into wealth-generating products and companies.

Universities and colleges and the "tech transfer" they can offer are increasingly important components of a modern economy. Health care; medical research; computer technology and design in its many facets; finance; global trade; and other significant categories of job creation are driving key segments of local economies.

Communities can become smarter by being devoted to increasing literacy and numeracy levels, growing local intellectual capacity, and partnering with colleges and universities. Smart municipalities understand that these commitments translate into a modern, dynamic civic culture of knowledge and innovation.

New CRINK sector jobs can drive many segments of a prosperous local economy. A strong job market, combined with a great lifestyle, encourages graduates to stay in that community. Municipalities need to support start-ups and young entrepreneurs because an appealing city attracts clusters of people dedicated to ideas and innovation. The cross-pollination of ideas and innovation spurs more productivity.

Successful CRINK economy examples are everywhere: Silicon Valley for software; Boston for science and medicine; New York for fashion, communications, finance, and much more; Waterloo for the computer/engineering sector that was sparked by Blackberry; Austin and Nashville for music and all those music industry spin-offs; the Research Triangle in North Carolina that has become perhaps the most important R&D district in the U.S.; Los Angeles for the sprawling entertainment sector, with its quantum leaps forward in technology, computer graphics, and artistic design that now feed a worldwide appetite.

Two common elements for these regions are a vibrant lifestyle and attractive, contemporary communities in which researchers, entrepreneurs, leaders, and dreamers want to live. This is crucial for local governments to understand.

The importance of building and re-establishing thriving cities is still emerging in many parts of North America. Faltering, crumbling cities in the U.S. "Rustbelt" get little attention until a catastrophe such as that experienced by Detroit. Lawyers, bondholders, and an angry public pick over the carcass that was once the proud Motor City. Derelict buildings make it look more like a war zone. Municipal leaders everywhere are asking themselves some very tough questions.

How Detroit may come back depends on many things; but, keys to its renaissance include: creation of a downtown hub of innovation and creativity; getting more people to live downtown; continuing to exploit assets such as the RiverWalk; urban farming; supporting the vibrant arts district headlined by the spectacular Detroit Institute of the Arts; capitalizing on the city's history of music; and encouraging the continued evolution of the auto companies as mobility suppliers, not just makers of cars.

Detroit also has to turn the street lights back on and do other basic local government tasks: get police responding more quickly to 911 calls; better public transit, so people can get to work; encourage young local entrepreneurs; fight blight in neighbourhoods (if a derelict building has to come down, get it done); support land banks; and commit to the restoration of this once-proud city. All this will demand attracting creative thinkers who will spur other entrepreneurial opportunities, innovative new businesses, job creation, and links with local educational institutions.

For Philadelphia, Bruce Katz and Jennifer Bradley (authors of *The Metropolitan Revolution*) offer ideas such an innovation district. This would combine cutting-edge companies with critical institutions (a university or college program, for example), and a mixed-use blend of office, retail, housing, and entrepreneurial companies and start-ups.

Getting local institutions working together and building momentum can be a pivotal point for communities. Creating incubator space for ideas, building strong networks both locally and internationally, fostering social networks, and accessing innovative minds and investor opportunities are all part of building a contemporary live/work/play district. This can provide a remarkable opportunity to repurpose a defunct neighbourhood.

Sometimes solutions will demand innovation from the local government. Melbourne, whose CRINK job sector has exploded, sets high standards for urban design, the sustainable retrofit of older buildings, and the preservation of heritage properties. The city quickly learned that the biggest barrier was access to capital by the owners of older buildings.

Melbourne thus initiated a new program with a bank: a green loan. The bank assesses the risk profile and makes a loan at better than commercial rates. The loan is repaid through the municipality as the city adds the loan to the building's property taxes. The bank now has security, so it is prepared to extend the loan; the owner gets cheaper money, so the building can be renovated and retrofitted; the building appreciates in value as tenants move in; and the city gets people living in a once-moribund block. The program achieves energy savings by demanding buildings be renovated to the latest green standards; heritage properties are preserved; and Melbourne eventually gets more tax revenue from these repurposed and improved buildings. It is a winning strategy that came from the local government looking at a problem through a different lens.

Pittsburgh, too, has reinvented itself in the last 40 years. At one time, the city was losing 4,000 jobs a month. Today, the city is a high-tech hub. It got there because local people came together, formed networks, beautified their city, and developed new hubs of commerce and technology. Much of the effort was led by young people. Communities need to exploit their young talent.

Even smaller communities can attract clusters of entrepreneurs and people engaged in a variety of job categories. To do so, they will have to offer a fully wired and modern communication and telecom system; social opportunities; a great quality of life; affordable housing; a culture that supports an international way of doing business; sustainable policies from local food to a green community; and a town or city dedicated to learning, innovation, and creativity.

Stratford, Ontario is a great example. The city of 35,000 is the home of the world-renowned Stratford Festival, a thriving food culture and restaurant scene, a new downtown university campus for digital media, and a computer centre fostering technology and innovation. It has been chosen as one of the world's Top 7 Intelligent Communities.

Smaller centres have to find their niche and then commit to re-making their community for the 21st century economy.

In Canada, the federal government remains without an urban agenda. It is seemingly quite blasé and indifferent to the plight of municipalities struggling with limited revenue sources and growing pleas for infrastructure investment. If Canada's economy is going to thrive, they need to help create sustainable, livable communities that offer a great quality of life.

In the United States, infrastructure deficits also grow steadily, and it often takes a bridge collapsing or a catastrophe of some other kind to awaken national media and lawmakers to the desperate plight of municipalities.

Communities in both countries look on impatiently and with disgust. Yet, at the same time, some local governments have been tormented by corruption, crime, malfeasance, and a decline in public trust.

The irony, of course, is that at a moment in time when many cities are truly emerging as the new stars in the galaxy, others are plagued by small thinking, petty politics, and corrupt or inept municipal officials. The result for *them*: a generation of decline and poverty.

It is a missed opportunity. Getting smart people to run for public office is difficult. We need to elevate our local leadership. Municipalities need to move forward confidently and assume a more equal role with their federal and provincial/state counterparts as we restructure the main orders of government for a more efficient, faster, and more progressive governance system.

Some local politicians don't yet grasp the grander opportunity that awaits smart, progressive communities. There is great complacency amongst those who don't understand how rapidly urban development is happening in other nations.

Those cities that are going to prosper in the future will need:

➤   strong leadership;

➤   great public spaces and places;

➤   prosperous economy;

➤   vibrant cultural direction;

➤   clear community focus; and

➤   great quality of life.

## Building the Infrastructure

Infrastructure investments are an urgent problem for a number of traditional western economies. The property tax base can't cover the cost of necessary urban infrastructure and our federal, provincial, and state governments have generally under-funded their municipalities. This situation will provide a growing advantage to brand new cities being built in China, Asia, Africa, India, and other nations.

To realistically estimate the infrastructure deficit, we need to take into consideration the electrical and telecommunications grids; the important "creative" elements such as libraries, parks, and public spaces and places that help make a community livable and appealing; the investments local governments are now expected to make toward the capital costs of universities, colleges, and hospitals; and the provincial and federal government responsibilities for *their* infrastructure, which directly impacts local prosperity (things like the TransCanada Highway, border crossings, harbours and bridges, and so on).

There is a very legitimate argument that Canada's true municipal infrastructure deficit is approaching a trillion dollars over the next 20 to 30 years. There is no conceivable way that local ratepayers can fund this on their property taxes. Nor can municipalities afford *new* infrastructure, such as servicing lands for employment growth and housing development.

The fear for smart municipal leaders is this: the gap is widening between brand new, sustainable and exciting cities in emerging regions of the world, and older cities facing crumbling infrastructure and hollowed-out downtowns in "western" nations. The competitive edge is shifting to newer cities and newer economies. Attractive cities with modern infrastructure will get the talent and economic investments that cities crave.

This is compounded by the rural to urban migration in China, Asia, South East Asia, Africa, and South America. An estimated one billion people will move (or be moved) over the next 25 to 30 years. The latest estimate is a cost of $50 trillion to build these new cities and expand existing infrastructure in older cities. We need to accommodate urban growth. Municipalities need to provide the power, water, high-speed train corridors, and the important amenities such as parks, public spaces, libraries, green oases, and the other elements that make communities livable.

No one knows how we're going to fund that. Especially for older communities.

Presumably, this demand will drive more P3s. In fact, it is quite likely that the private sector will assume an even greater role in building new cities and communities. Songdo, South Korea is a 10-year-old, $40B city built almost entirely by private money. This dynamic business and financial centre has 300,000 people working there daily.

Private investments will require new thinking from planners and architects about how to use the public realm. It will mean more neighbourhoods that are largely self contained. They will be walkable, greener, less reliant on cars, and more dependent on public transportation. Local food concerns will be supported. Greater density will mean higher buildings, which in turn will mean sidewalk traffic and design will become much more important.

In South African cities (which face torrential downpours and great heat) Jack Diamond notes that commercial areas were mandated to provide coverage so the public would have protection from rain and sun.

"In Canada, why don't we mandate protection from snow and ice? I'm curious why we don't, because the sidewalk is North America's most important public space. It's where the pedestrian is, it's where movement takes place, but we make them mean," he says.

Some cities don't. Washington, DC is an example – sidewalks are very wide, so they can landscape them.

Jack Diamond suggests other concepts such as street narrowing, instead of street widening, because it slows traffic; and sidewalks designed to provide coverage for pedestrians. "Good cities provide generosity; bad cities provide meanness in their public spaces," he says.

How communities use, abuse, and develop their public spaces will come under greater scrutiny. The public will demand it, because that will be where they spend much of their social and leisure time. Nations and municipalities will have to find trillions of dollars for urban infrastructure investments in the next 25 years.

## New Urbanism

There are a number of common elements to "new urbanism" and the placemaking elements that go into such neighbourhoods:

➤ mixed-use communities (self-contained with parks, shopping, and work that is often close enough for walking or cycling);

➤ much less reliance/usage of automobiles;

➤ public transportation that is easily accessible and designed for high usage;

➤ mid- and high-rise developments;

➤ narrow streets, some with back alleys, so traffic is calmed;

➤ smaller building lots and front porches to encourage neighbours and families to interact; and

➤ compact and sustainable design.

To some people, this new urbanism is a return to the pre-1940s era in North America, perhaps similar to what has been built for centuries in Europe.

The use of the streets and sidewalks present fascinating design opportunities for planners. Sometimes known as "Complete Streets," it raises the critical question of who owns the street. Cars or people?

Jennifer Keesmaat points to an important debate among planners today: "Discussion is starting about use of streets, their design, their future ... are streets places to move cars, or are they places where people gather? Where pedestrians belong? Where cyclists belong?"

She continues, "The powerful part of the Complete Streets exercise is that not only is it going to provide specific direction to our transportation engineer when we're implementing new streetscape design, but it shifts the paradigm in how we conceive of and understand the role of street infrastructure that already exists. Once people start to experience it, it can help to move minds, get people to think differently."

It can also change a community's public places and spaces. Times Square in New York is a great example. The city reclaimed the street for pedestrians and strictly limited vehicle traffic. Today, it is a thriving, 24-hour-a-day hub where pedestrians roam, bright lights explode, the action on the street never stops, and the biggest companies in the world vie for your attention.

In a 2013 TED talk, NYC transportation commissioner Janette Sadik-Kahn said, "Streets are some of the most valuable assets a city has, and yet it is an asset hidden in plain sight. You can remake your streets quickly, inexpensively, it can provide immediate benefits, and it can be quite popular. You just need to look at them a little differently."

She continued, revealing the city's actions and success: "We've moved very quickly. Instead of waiting through years of planning studies and computer models to get something done, we've done it with paint and temporary materials. And the proof is not in a computer model. It is in the real world performance of the street. You can have fun with paint. All told, we've created over 50 pedestrian plazas in all five boroughs across the city. We've repurposed 26 acres of active car lanes and turned them into new pedestrian space."

Larry Beasley is blunt about how important this discussion is for cities. "In every smart city, you have to draw the line about how much you're going to dedicate to the car. It has everything to do with the demands of all of the other uses of public space. You just have to ignore the demands of the car at some point."

This car versus pedestrian debate opens the door for new thinking for planners and designers. The "lighter/quicker/cheaper" approach allows a municipality to "try out" new ideas and shift public perception – all for a minimal cost.

*Leading cities like Melbourne and Auckland understand that sidewalks are one of their greatest assets: wide, tree-lined, animated, allowing cafes, improving how buildings interface with the sidewalk. Some cities even "roof" sidewalks to provide protection for pedestrians, or heat them to ensure safe winter passage.*

Another example comes from downtown Toronto in the summer of 2012, when enterprising people took over two lanes of Yonge Street and created a parkette. They also did programming (*full disclosure: I spoke at this event*) and provided a café/social media location to encourage random encounters.

"Celebrate Yonge Street tracked the number of pedestrians and the impact on retail. The project was really the 'lighter/quicker/cheaper' approach to the public realm, which is 'let's not get hung up on changing the curbs; let's just throw out some planters and let people know this is going to be a great public space'," notes Jennifer Keesmaat.

Reaction to the event was generally positive. Creative thinking can change a downtown street, corridor, or area – with minimal cost to the city and minimal disruption to the community.

Rapidly emerging today is the LEED for Neighbourhood Development program (LEED ND), which takes the traditional LEED rating system beyond the building scale, and provides best practices and standards that can be applied to neighbourhoods (either new or refurbished), integrating the concepts of new urbanism, healthy communities, green building design, smart growth, and holistic community planning.

Most communities are searching for ways to freshen neighbour-hoods and downtown streets. But, they must overcome their fear of "new and different" when it comes to planning and use of the public realm. A community's spaces are one of its greatest assets. How to use and animate those spaces are great challenges as urban design-ers and planners reshape our spatial thinking. Innovative projects like Celebrate Yonge Street prove that municipal planners and com-munity activists can try out new ideas in real time and real place.

Potential sites can be anything – from unused roof-tops that can become green spaces to tiny, empty lots that can be redeveloped as "pocket parks." It requires understanding the importance of side-walks and making them welcoming and friendly. It requires adopt-ing standards that make buildings more compatible with their street, perhaps through setbacks or tapering.

We need to rethink streets and who owns them. We need to focus on the people who live, work, and play in the community and then adapt the physical realm to the contemporary needs of residents and visitors.

What we build in those public spaces makes an important statement about our communities.

Enter the architects and their imagination.

# CHAPTER 7

# THE POWER OF ARCHITECTURE

*"Every city is a living body." – St. Augustine*

Great architecture is that perfect connection between art and engineering; it creates beauty that is functional. Asking where the inspiration comes from is akin to asking how Mozart composed music. Brilliant architects just see space differently.

Many of the world's most important advancements have come because of astonishing leaps in design, construction, and engineering: the pyramids; the Mayan temples; the Forbidden City; the glory of the Taj Mahal; the great cathedrals of Europe in the Renaissance period; the Parthenon; the wondrous river-spanning aqueducts of the Roman Empire.

Imagine being the architects in Constantinople in 532, ordered by the emperor to design and build a cathedral. What emerged from their fertile minds was the Hagia Sophia, which for a thousand years reigned as the most magnificent cathedral in the world. It became a mosque, and is now a museum. The architects' astonishing design and building techniques, using vaults and semi-domes that combine to support a glorious central dome over 100 feet in diameter, represented a significant breakthrough in architecture and construction. To this day, awed tourists come to admire the basilica, the marble pillars, the gold and precious stones, and the artwork. This is the power of great architecture.

Perhaps a community's architecture is what makes the most significant statement about that community. Does it encourage elegant, lasting design? Does it support monuments to innovation and creativity? Does it understand the link between design and living? Does it demand a higher standard for its public and private spaces and places?

Or, does it allow badly-designed buildings that are a strident, brutal interruption to a lovely streetscape? Structures that don't fit with the neighbourhood? That send out a negative, dark vibe?

There are many elements to good urban design, but the constant is the imagination and creativity of the architect. We instinctively like a beautifully-designed building or house. We feel good.

Historically, great buildings were almost always ordered by the government, the church, or rich patrons: palaces, cathedrals, libraries, coliseums, and religious ceremonial sites, for example.

In some ways, not that much has changed – yet *everything* has changed.

For local governments today, money is the culprit. But, more than that, some cities and countries simply have a historic commitment to great design that is rooted deeply in their culture. That passion is absent in many communities today.

Eddie Friel understands this dichotomy. "Very few municipal structures in North America are memorable. There is a greater debate about the nature of places and the livability, as opposed to the structures we put up."

He then offers a penetrating question for municipal leaders to ponder: "What is different about this place?" In other words, how do cities separate themselves? How do they become distinctive in an era when gateways to cities are often shopping centres, cheap motels, and fast food restaurants ... and they all look the same?

"In the 70s, design was horrible, just horrible," says architect John Nicholson.

Jeff Fielding continues the theme. "Public spaces in North America evolved because of suburban lifestyle, drive-throughs, and cars. In Europe, there was always more effort on creating intimate spaces in the fabric of community, and celebrating the history of public venues. Europe has had the advantage of many centuries of growing its urban environment. It had a core urban fabric in place. North America is only 200 years old, and the last hundred years have been dominated by the car."

It seems apparent why great government designs have fallen on hard times. "It's a money thing," says Jeff Fielding clearly. "Certainly since the 80s, we've not invested in quality structures, places, design. The money in local government hasn't been there. That won't change. In fact, I see it going the other way. 'Nice to have things' fall to the bottom in public surveys."

Urban design is all about how municipalities control, use, and abuse the public realm. "Cities are losing on their public environment," warns Larry Beasley. "There are competitive advantages to improving the quality of the public realm. There is a real insensitivity to public needs, and that comes down to money."

"It is not either/or," stresses Eddie Friel. "[Municipalities need a] sense of place. Quality of place must be identified to persuade people of the need to invest in infrastructure and the need to generate wealth. Investment in public places and spaces can help to attract people, generate wealth ... public spaces and places are part of that."

This is a clear message that many politicians from all orders of government simply do not get today. In an increasingly disposable society, we are rarely leaving a legacy of great design or intriguing architecture.

There is an economic payback from investing in outstanding design. A thousand years from now, are people going to come to gaze in wonder at your city's ... well, anything?

In the sixth century, somehow, against stunning hardships and seemingly insurmountable problems, they designed and built the Hagia Sophia; in the 21st century, what do we build that is memorable and lasting?

## Heritage Factor

Perhaps it has been the lack of interesting design from governments over the past decades that has helped to spur the recent interest in saving and re-purposing heritage buildings and properties.

Communities are recognizing that preserving heritage offers a distinctive difference between a particular neighbourhood or town and all the others. Salvaging heritage buildings that have been abandoned is sometimes the catalyst to bring that area back to life.

Often, that initial discovery is made by artists and artisans who are looking for cheap, chic places for their art and lifestyle to flourish. Once they get rooted, coffee shops and music bars slide in, abandoned buildings get renovated into interesting housing or hotels, restaurants open and are discovered, and suddenly a neighbourhood is hot.

Tim Jones, CEO of Artscape in Toronto, is a dynamic leader in linking neighbourhoods, real estate development, and the creative community. He made this point as a guest contributor in the 2009 book *Cultural Planning for Creative Communities*:

"Conventional wisdom about the plight of artists in the path of gentrifying neighbourhoods is that very little can be done about it. In the urban development community, it is common to hear planners, developers, and city councillors talk about the displacement of artists from the places that they enlivened as part of the natural city evolution process. But, it is hardly appropriate to celebrate a phenomenon where the group that adds so much to property values consistently gets the raw end of the deal in the real estate market. Their nomadic condition results in repeated workplace disruption, and being relegated to the margins of urban life, where they are disconnected from other creative people and the marketplace. This cycle not only perpetuates the poverty of artists, but it diminishes their capacity to add value over time to local communities. If the development community took a longer view of the situation, it would realize the people being displaced were essential in retaining the vibrancy and authenticity of neighbourhoods and, therefore, in preserving real estate values."

*The famous Blue Mosque in Istanbul, started in 1609, is an example of stunning architectural achievements that can set a city apart.*

Solutions are emerging. Providing artists with live/work/display space in new developments is one answer. Allocating studio space for artisans and creators in commercial/industrial developments or re-developments is another. Repurposing abandoned properties, as Artscape did so brilliantly with the Wychwood Barns project in Toronto (turning an old, closed bus barn into a thriving community centre that provides everything from herb gardens and community bake ovens to studio space for creators) is another. Artscape was an early driver in the transformation of the Distillery District (now a hot spot in the Toronto diaspora) when it worked to provide below-market rents to artists to get them established in this emerging public place. That helped create the vibe of a successful development.

Globally, there are many examples of the glorious opportunity to link heritage redevelopment, the arts/creative industry, real estate development, and neighbourhood improvement. They include Beijing's 798 District; London, England's ACME and Space; the arts district in Minneapolis; and Shanghai's development of an abandoned factory district into a dynamic arts community known as M50.

The results of such initiatives have been consistent – vibrant new neighbourhoods, often utilizing architectural innovation to help salvage abandoned heritage buildings and repurpose them. The upshot of intrepid design and attracting creative minds is a fun and exciting new destination for locals and tourists alike. Municipalities, meanwhile, enjoy the benefits from thriving new districts that were once derelict properties. And, of course, the added bonus of new tax revenue.

## Palette of Colours

A decade ago, the new mayor of the tired old city of Tirana, Albania (for half a century the grey, oppressed, and depressed capital of this former Soviet bloc nation) took a bold step: he bought a bunch of paint and had artists decorate the town with bright colours, bold artistic murals, and geometric designs. This new kaleidoscopic effect brought back life and energy to the community – a spirit that endures today.

Remember what Tessa Virtue said about cities – how colour speaks, how it affects a visitor's perception, how the grey of a polluted industrial city in China compares against the colours and vibrancy of Paris. Planners, architects, and civic officials need to understand the use and importance of colour in public places and spaces to help create an image for the community.

The hues, shades, and tones of the palette of colours for an architect are a critical part of great design – as are texture, shading, and sunlight.

Colours have a psychological impact. Blues are often the most preferred colour for men; blues confer a feeling of peace, security, and comfort, stimulating the mind while offering calm and serenity. Red is a powerful colour that is strong, passionate, exciting; women love red shades. Black is sophisticated and authoritative; grey is wisdom; white is neutral. Brown, green, and the earth tones are warm and friendly, which is why they are often used in offices and businesses. Purple has a regal history.

Designers are well aware of the effect colours have on people. Bold architects are beginning to clad their buildings in robust reds, terra cotta, and saffron. They know how these colours impact people psychologically. They help to set a mood and send a message. In public spaces, they create a feeling, a vibe, which visitors and tourists quickly absorb.

At the Beijing Olympics, the aquatic events were held in the Water Cube. Designed as a very modern structure, but based upon Chinese history, the membrane technology was groundbreaking – the walls changed colour. Outside the aquatic centre was a large open public space that included dancing waters, music, and a location for spontaneous celebrations. The colourful display quickly became a popular gathering place for people from around the world. Much of the talk from a hundred different cultures was about the design and use of that public space. It created a common shared experience, and out of that chatter grew friendships that circled the globe.

That is the benefit of unique public spaces: social interaction and shared experiences.

Many communities are now repurposing building walls, railway overpasses, and other public and private spaces to create colourful and interesting murals. While these initiatives are sometimes a reaction to graffiti, they are often becoming a planned addition to enhance a community's colourful public face. They may help to tell the story of a community's heritage, or celebrate its diversity and culture.

## Water, Wood & Glass

Architects, builders, and designers must know the impact of the building materials they choose. These elements, too, send a message. Elected officials need to better appreciate and understand the nuances of colour and material in buildings and in/on public places and spaces, so they can demand more creativity and bolder design.

Magnificent glass domes have been used effectively to make dramatic statements in buildings. They bring the outside inside, allowing the sun to sparkle, and colouring the corners of our lives. They provide a window out, and sometimes a look in, and can have a dazzling impact.

The glass pyramid at the Louvre Museum in Paris makes a dramatic, one-of-a-kind design statement. I.M. Pei's entrance to one of the world's greatest museums in one of its most fashionable cities proves the impact and power of imaginative design. The controversial project has intrigued millions; and, once again, the power of audacious architecture to inspire and invigorate is evident.

At Harbourfront in Toronto, a three-storey wall of glass is the brilliant design leading into a parking area – yes, an underground parking garage. Light is refracted and then channeled down through the garage, resulting in a dramatic entrance.

The Great Court at the British Museum in London is a glass-domed space that opened in 2000, creating the largest covered public space in Europe. The gorgeous glass roof brought the courtyard that had been almost lost for 150 years back to life. The museum was then able to develop new spaces and places under the dome and expand the museum experience.

Milan's Galleria Vittorio Emanuele II is an architectural gem of a shopping centre. Building on Milan's history of art and design, the street and piazza offer visitors an experience that delights as they stroll under the towering glass peaks. The city claims a great history of art, architecture, and design that contribute to the richness of Milan's textures. The glass-enclosed shopping area builds upon that reputation, and has become a major destination.

North American cities have little to match such striking design in and of the public realm. And, when municipalities don't display their own design vigour and capacity, the private sector has little incentive to innovate either. Eras of tired, dull grey concrete highrise apartments and towers in urban areas have today given way to downtown glass and steel condos that many feel have become equally boring and pedestrian.

But, happily, glimmers of hope are appearing. Use of wood in buildings, even high-rises, is emerging (appropriate, given Canada's vast forests – one of this country's great resources). Public buildings in British Columbia and Northern Ontario, among others, are increasingly using local forestry products. Wood is warm and familiar, it absorbs sound, and people like its look and feel.

Canada's new school of architecture opened at Laurentian University in Sudbury, Ontario in 2013. The college's home is a wooden, century-old former railway shed and telegraph building. Fittingly, the new structure uses wood as the primary construction material.

The Richmond Olympic Oval in British Columbia was the site of long-track speed skating competitions at the 2010 Vancouver Olympics. It has now been repurposed as an international centre for excellence for sports, health, and fitness. The venue garnered more than 30 awards for its soaring architecture, sustainability, and construction. The arches for the Olympic Oval are the longest spanning hybrid steel-wood arches in the world. The wood for the ceiling came primarily from lumber reclaimed after B.C.'s devastating pine beetle infestation.

On the shores of Lake Superior, a marvellous piece of public art, "Gathering Circle" by Ojibway architectural graduate Ryan Gorrie, uses traditional bentwood spruce. It is the centrepiece of a larger project to reclaim old industrial land in Thunder Bay, Ontario and create a healthy new waterfront park.

In Melbourne, Australia, a 10-storey apartment is being built from cross-laminated timber. In addition to a beautiful look, it is more energy efficient and will produce less carbon dioxide emissions than a traditional concrete/steel structure.

Stone is another great Canadian resource that is increasingly being used by clever designers and architects. It provides unique colours and textures both inside and outside buildings.

Water, too, is an element that communities are discovering. People like water features – they soothe, provide a cool space to sit or play, and offer a tranquil respite from our busy lives. Developers in Vancouver have often enhanced the public and private realm by including lovely cascading water features as part of the décor of residential and office complexes. Fountains have long been a feature of European piazzas and public squares, and are growing in popularity across North America as well. Indoors or out, water features (often with special lighting to provoke even greater reactions) are an appealing design element.

Often tied closely to these water features are "green walls," such as that found in the Cambridge, Ontario city hall. Soaring several stories through an atrium, green walls are environmentally friendly and support a municipal sustainability agenda. So do green roofs on civic buildings. These initiatives are becoming more common as municipalities show leadership on ecological matters through better architectural design and use of public places and spaces.

## Changing the Municipal Design Process

Some municipalities are responding to the growing demand for better urban design by taking action and raising that bar. More councillors are beginning to understand their rare opportunity to enhance the public realm by insisting on innovative designs and features.

Some cities have developed urban design award programs to celebrate this creativity. Peer-review panels are being established in many communities to demand higher levels of design and innovation. Questions about landscaping, lighting, colours, and clerestories are now part of robust conversations taking place inside some council chambers.

The public is getting increasingly engaged and immersed in the process. Lonely protests over lousy, boring design that once came from isolated groups or individuals are now being replaced by engaged dialogue with communities and organizations pressing for better urban design. There is hope emerging for a new era of innovation. People are beginning to understand – even insist – that government projects are architecturally significant.

The problem is financing. How to pay for these projects. There remains a core of taxpayers opposed to public money being spent on ... well, pretty much anything. Politicians rarely show the leadership that is demanded to push for interesting and unique design in public buildings.

Perhaps our society in many North American communities, our municipal culture if you will, is still not yet far enough advanced. What trade-offs are we prepared to make with limited public budgets? Does innovative design have to cost more? Should governments be investing a bit more to ensure an architecturally-significant building with environmentally-leading technology? And, can those buildings be designed to enhance a city's culture? Is that a good investment of public money?

Municipalities need to convince skeptics that investments in design and innovation have an economic payback because they help to shape and build a more prosperous community that can better compete in this 21st century global economy and hunt for talent.

The battle is far from over, but it is a fight worth fighting.

## Architects, Planners, and Our Changing Environment

Municipalities and local politicians are recognizing that architecture, design, climate change, and how their communities are built are inextricably linked. The results directly impact the use of the public realm. That has implications for the health of residents, how residents and tourists will gather and socialize, and the overall image and impressions of the community.

Copenhagen, Denmark gives priority to bicycles over cars. Toronto will have the most green roofs of any city in the world within four years. Vancouver is committed to becoming the greenest city in the world by 2020. Other cities now offer development charge rebates for projects that attain certain green standards in design and building.

Important questions need to be asked by councillors: Are streets and neighbourhoods designed to be people friendly or vehicle dominated? Are building materials close, or do they have to be shipped thousands of miles? Can the project recycle wastewater and/or garbage to generate heat and electricity? Should the design of buildings be mandated to provide secure bicycle parking and change rooms for cyclists? What "green" features are in the building's design and materials? Does the building concept meet Green Globe or LEED standards?

The external design of a building is as important as the internal components. What can the landscaping do to contribute positively to the environment? How can it help to cool the building entrance and the sidewalk? What native species can be planted? Is there space for a community garden? Can solar panels be added to a roof or patio?

Automated buildings that "think" (in other words, that automatically adjust to sunlight, issue fire warnings, shut off lights and heat when people aren't in a room, lead people to safety in an emergency) are, by definition, more environmentally friendly and use less energy.

How can buildings and their design strengthen opportunities for walking and support a healthier lifestyle? Encourage casual socializing? Support the local food agenda? Ensure full accessibility? Offer full and flexible technology tools and ease of access throughout offices and floors? Integrate with the sidewalk?

These are the new design standards and best practices that skilled architects must now support, builders must construct, and municipalities must demand.

How cities develop a more harmonious blend of public places and spaces, and link the private realm, is going to become one of the great challenges of the 21st century for urban planners, developers, architects, and builders.

There are dozens (maybe even hundreds) of small spaces in every town or city where the public and private realms intersect – the "in between" spaces. How those spaces are used is of great significance in shaping a city or neighbourhood.

Can little parks be created from small empty lots? Can plopping down a park bench or two suddenly result in a new meeting place for those living in that neighbourhood? Can cleaning up an empty lot spark a movement by local residents to take back those filthy little corners of a street that everybody hates? Can doing something with dark, closed stores and windows spark a safer feeling on the street? Can allowing cafes to put up tables on sidewalks and even parking places on the street help to slow traffic and promote strolling and socializing?

These ideas and many more suggest small, easy things that municipalities can do. The public and private realm can come together. A few trees and a community garden planted in what was an abandoned gas station suddenly changes the feel of that corner – something that Communities in Bloom participants have known for years, beautifying their communities and making real social change happen on the streets ... with plants.

## Healthier Cities

Designing healthier cities is of paramount importance. We need to encourage and support activity, walkability, socializing, and access to local food. Planning decisions have a direct impact on the health of local residents.

Communities striving for better urban design have to consider the growing impact of climate change. Wind storms. More extreme heat and cold. Floods have ravaged communities in many places in recent years; 100-year flood events seem to be occurring with alarming regularity. Tornadoes, hurricanes, and fierce storms lash towns and coastal areas. It is clear that the Arctic ice cover is diminishing. Climate change is happening, and evidence points to use and misuse of the planet by the human race as the primary cause.

We need to reduce GHGs and think hard about our lifestyle. Certainly, North Americans have enjoyed a rather dissolute lifestyle for many decades. My purpose is not to moralize – I have no right to do so – but, rather, to observe practically that the realities of life today have placed governments of all orders (but particularly municipalities) squarely in the crosshairs for better understanding and dealing with the impact of climate change. They need to take action.

In 2014, the World Health Organization (WHO) reported that about seven million people died in 2012 as a result of exposure to air pollution. Air pollution is now identified as the world's largest single environmental health risk. And, cities emit about 80 percent of all global carbon dioxide emissions.

As millions of people pour into new cities in China, India, Africa, and other areas, the smog-choking lifestyle that has long been tolerated there simply will *not* be in the future. If the emerging middle class in these countries adopts a more western lifestyle (for example, getting their own automobiles), the implications for future air quality will be staggering.

"The fate of the earth's climate basically hinges on what we do with our cities," according to the Tyndall Centre for Climate Change Research located in Great Britain.

As UN-Habitat points out, 95 percent of the expected global population growth will come from cities in the developing world over the next two decades. This higher density also means increases in urban poverty: about 75 percent of the world's poorest live in cities.

The WHO predicts that two billion people will live in slums in big cities. The health risks for families will increase. According to a UN report, the population growth in cities in the developing world "has outpaced the ability to provide vital infrastructure and services."

It all adds up to a potential environmental, health, and human disaster.

## While Countries Talk, Communities Transform

Forget the apparently useless international accords on climate change. Action is going to come down to the protection of our streets, homes, and rivers in our cities by local governments, and the direct intervention and environmental leadership of community residents and businesses. That is why we are developing new building and design techniques and policies. That is why municipalities have been thrust into the leadership position on developing more sustainable communities.

The need for sustainability is going to drive the demand for greater action and change. The impact will be felt first and most effectively at the local government level.

Municipalities need to work with their sister or partner communities in other corners of the world to promote greener municipal techniques and initiatives. In fact, municipalities may soon become the leaders in green projects, and the federal governments' inertia may be replaced by citizens and local leaders forming partnerships – both locally and globally.

Melbourne has replaced 30 hectares of asphalt. It is creating new green spaces. The city is committed to planting 3,000 extra trees a year in their downtown. Why? Mapping shows their central city is five degrees hotter than the suburbs; by planting trees, it will cool the central city by four degrees – with subsequent savings in energy.

Local government simply moves faster than other orders of government. They have the capacity and the flexibility to set impressive local targets and actions for improving sustainability and environmentally-friendly actions. Destination charges for cars entering a downtown, as an example, have an immediate impact on air pollution.

This is another reason why cities are becoming so important, and why global partnerships between communities will become even more critical. New ideas on sustainability need to be explored and shared. Surely cities in emerging markets can benefit from some of the lessons already experienced by cities in developed economies.

North American cities, for example, are huge consumers of electricity. They generate substantial GHGs. They are sources of pollution for our water and land. Recyclables are poured into landfills. We throw away 30 to 40 percent of the food produced. That must change.

Demands for improvement will only accelerate. North American municipal and community leaders have to find a way to help cities and families in developing markets to understand the urgency and importance of environmental issues. The challenge will be that these emerging markets are trying desperately to provide jobs and a brighter future for the millions who are pouring into their new cities. The battle between jobs, economic development, industrial progress, and the realities of climate change and environmental issues is far from over.

It will not be an easy or a quick fix. North American lifestyles are comfortable and well established, and there is little sense of urgency for most. Urban design and lifestyle changes will most likely come incrementally, and civic and community leaders will have to nudge and pull residents along the path.

We'll need new thinking about downtown streets, public transportation, and green spaces. We'll need fresh urban design for street traffic and sidewalk usage. We'll discover better use of building materials and techniques that are more eco-friendly. There will be a slow public movement towards absorbing the problems and supporting the solutions.

Our efforts must stretch out to mayors, councillors, and community leaders from around the world. Municipalities need to link with each other, work together, and design effective solutions to help both developed and emerging communities become more sustainable. Architects and urban planners will also be at the forefront of this rethinking.

Perhaps a good place to start is in the suburbs. They are emerging as the greatest challenge facing our new generation of planners, architects, and civic champions.

# CHAPTER 8

# SAVING OUR SUBURBS

*"Suburb: a place that isn't a city, isn't country, and isn't tolerable."*
*– Mignon McLaughlin, in The Second Neurotic's Notebook, 1966*

About 15 to 20 percent of Canadians live in dense urban cores.

About 15 to 20 percent live in smaller communities and rural areas.

About 60 percent live in some form of the suburbs.

Life in the suburbs has been driven by sprawl, cars, highways, sewer and water trunk lines, aggressive developers, and families seeking an affordable house and relief from urban blight.

Despite the popularization of the "suburban life" that has hung on since the 1950s, some dreadful planning choices were made by municipalities in developing suburbs. A lot of trees got bulldozed, hills and ravines got leveled, and big chunks of the eco-system got paved.

"Planners did some terrible things – no sidewalks, no connectivity, car-focused, lack of trees/green space," says architect John Nicholson. "People wanted to exit a city centre, which in turn hollowed-out downtowns."

The car-focused planning and design of suburbs has continued to make walking difficult in many suburban neighbourhoods. Shockingly, only about 12 percent of children in North America walk or bike to school (for a variety of reasons). That's bad for their health and bad for our environment.

Financially, sprawl is very costly for municipalities. Servicing these lands is expensive, especially if developers can convince weak councils to "leap frog" development. Environmental issues are a growing concern for the ongoing viability of suburbs; but, sustainability has not been a driving force for most suburban neighbourhoods until recent years.

Community leaders today better understand the toll it takes to support a vehicle-driven suburban development and the impact that decision has on the environment. There is a concerted effort in some smart cities to dramatically improve suburban design. They are insisting that developers use natural features, incorporate green spaces into the subdivision's design, build in environmentally-friendly concepts such as walking and bike paths, and make stormwater ponds attractive features.

Lifestyle issues and our changing family structure are also key factors in rethinking our suburbs. People are marrying later. Forty percent of people in their 20s still live at home. Some families are now hosting three or four generations in the same household. Neighbourhoods are much more diverse and cosmopolitan. Quality of life concerns are making many rethink the big house, multiple cars, and a two-hour daily commute.

Big box stores abound in suburban areas, while local food outlets are scarce. The design of cul-de-sacs and street patterns have caused monumental problems for access, servicing, and sustainability. Limited public transportation has exacerbated the car problems. Some suburban homeowners today are increasingly worried about getting stuck in a big, mortgage-devouring house while baby boomers age and retire and society drifts toward smaller homes and denser urban life.

Yet, cities haven't given much thought or applied innovative design to suburbs. That is a problem, and it is becoming more urgent.

"We have to change our suburbs," says Larry Beasley bluntly. And, in a moment of brutal introspection, he continues, "In the last generation or so, we've been focusing on the more urban areas of our cities. If you look at a subdivision being laid out in a suburban area anywhere in Canada today, it probably is applying the standards generated in the late 1950s. We haven't put much creative thought into suburbs. The second thing is, we've been living a very peculiar illusion in this country, which is that all the consumers that go to suburbs, and that's the majority of Canadians, love them. Well, it turns out that they don't love them. They just think they are their only choice to those horrible, dense, tall, scary core cities that planners have been creating for the last 25 years. I was one of the leaders. We were revitalizing cities that were dying. The problem is that no one has paid much attention to suburbs. I tell young planners, now it is your challenge and if your generation doesn't fix it, the nation is in trouble. We'll never be green unless we transform our suburbs. And, part of that is about placemaking and it's about some forms of compactness and it's about creating places people want to invest in and stay in. It's all the things we know about, and it has to happen."

Defining the challenges and problems of suburban life is increasingly a focus for civic leaders.

Jack Diamond offers an equally candid assessment of suburban life and the growing appeal of urban living. "The good news is that the flight to the suburbs has been reversed, or at least stayed. There is a new generation of people who don't want to commute. They want the amenities and benefits of urban life."

There is a different social environment in a suburban development. "The upside of the suburb is that it is a good place for child rearing. You have privacy of ownership. You have real security against public invasion of your space. For example, a porch works because it is the intermediary between the public and your private space. You can engage someone on the porch without inviting them in to your home. However, suburban life lacks the very thing we're talking about – where the community coalesces, comes together, and there is communal life," he says.

Our social structure is impacted by where people choose to live. Jack Diamond presents a fascinating theory about a switch in residential living: "The poor have migrated to the suburb cluster locations and they are no longer in the inner city because it is too expensive. While the good news is that there's an in-flow into the city,

the bad news is that it is a small segment of the population – it is
the young, those in career formation, usually without children. They
don't engage in the community as much as people with children.
The young people and condominium owners are so engaged in their
career formation and their lives they have little stake on the streets."

Municipal politicians, urban designers, and planners are beginning
to turn their heads to the problems of suburbs, and the resulting sustainability and lifestyle issues. There can be "good density" in the
suburbs. Innovative ideas are crucial.

I asked Larry Beasley whether change will be driven by economic
issues, sustainability issues, or people issues. His answer was il-
luminating: "Most planners would say it is going to be driven by
sustainability issues. I believe it's going to be driven by quality of
life issues. You have to take the consumer view. If we focus on their
needs, their quality of life, we can insinuate all the things we need
for a green agenda and other things into new models that I think
will be bought because consumers want them. I believe a slight shift
in consumer preferences is much more powerful than the strongest
adopted public policy."

Municipal rules can be restrictive rather than encouraging innovation. "In one Canadian city, we were talking about [how cool it
would be] to have neighbourhoods, so-called streetcar suburbs, that
were very sustainable, and learn from them. But, when we met with
developers, they said to try something like a sustainable suburb is
illegal, we can't afford to take that [risk]," he observed with some
disappointment.

The reasons are complex and vary between communities, but as
he explains, "A mature streetcar suburb has narrower streets than
allowed by current standards. It has more housing diversity than
now allowed by exclusionary suburban zoning. It uses property in
a more intensive and diverse way than would be allowed by current zoning or building codes. It usually has smaller lot sizes than
suburban standards and back lanes that are in some cases popu-
lated with infill units facing the lane. Post-war suburbs usually do
not have back lanes and the zoning would not allow a secondary
residential building.

[The streetcar suburb] can be economically served by transit because its density is high enough and its footprint is low enough to
offer enough transit riders very close by. That is not the case with
the sprawling postwar suburb. [Older neighbourhoods have] tight
street-oriented and sometimes multi-storey retail with modest parking, whereas the postwar suburb has a sea of parking because the
by-laws require it and the mass-market retail format insists on it
even though those parking lots are often empty. [These are] just several of the relevant reasons why it would be illegal to build at this
point and require sweeping changes in the laws that developers cannot facilitate on their own."

Fundamental restructuring of suburbs may be forced on cities. There
are declines in retail store traffic as internet shopping becomes more
prevalent. That shift could have dramatic implications for suburban
malls and big box stores. Having acres of empty parking lots and
abandoned retail outlets is a potential nightmare for municipalities.

These various suburban issues combine to create a huge opportunity. What we're missing are ideas. That is the challenge facing the
next generation of planners and community leaders.

Suburbs have usually failed to offer a "main street" that is treed,
walkable, pleasant, and comfortable. Instead, vehicles scoot through
wide arterial roads, often at a high speed, and there is little connection to life on the street. There is no "sense of community." Cities
have raised expectations about suburban life that are not always
fulfilled.

Jennifer Keesmaat faces these critical issues every day. "A lot of
people love their suburbs and it is imperative to acknowledge that;
unfortunately, they don't love all of the suburbs because there are
consequences that come with suburban sprawl, which include long
commutes, not having access to great public transit ... these are tensions we see. People want a low density neighbourhood, but they
also want access to a subway! There is disconnect between urban
form and structure and what's achievable. There is a reason we put
subways into high-density spaces. You can't live on an acre lot and
have a subway outside your door. It is not sustainable and it is not
good planning."

In Toronto, 81 percent of growth is happening in the small area of the downtown core, notes Jennifer Keesmaat. "With that density, the city has the need and resources to focus on urban places and invest in the public realm, whereas we don't have that same justification in our more suburban environments. The challenge in Toronto is that a lot of those suburban communities built in the 50s and 60s, their infrastructure is now coming due, but is not being revitalized."

Suburbs themselves are multi-layered, and that is difficult to understand. Suburbs are not one homogenous entity.

"It is hard to speak of the suburbs as one thing because there's so much diversity. [In Toronto] we have 13 priority neighbourhoods, which are concrete towers that were built in the 60s and 70s to be middle class housing that now have become places with the highest crime and most poverty. A lot of those communities are in our suburbs. We have towers with a lot of density, but we also have low rise communities that are single-family dwellings that are being adapted and changed into group homes and rooming houses. Those environments are changing and are very different from the 1950s idea of what they were intended to be. Then we have stable suburban communities, leafy green, prosperous, often the housing stock is extremely well maintained ... these dynamics are very different," Jennifer Keesmaat concludes.

What have sometimes emerged are small, unique neighbourhoods that have survived and developed on their own, perhaps coming from older settlements that were annexed but managed to keep their local character. These places usually display key attributes of sustainable, livable neighbourhoods (narrower streets, walkability, local shops and cafes, trees, street furniture, and tradition – such as an ice cream store that is a family favorite, or a park that attracts generations). These little gems are different from modern suburbs that too often only offer speeding traffic and isolation, and fail the test of connectivity – both human and physical.

Rethinking the traditional design of suburbs is emerging as a critical opportunity for cities that want to develop a sustainable quality of life for their residents.

"The best thing a planner has to say about suburbs is transit-oriented development," says Larry Beasley. He notes that "80 percent of the 60 percent who live in suburbs do not want higher-density housing. We can talk about gentle densification and clustering around public places. For the country, it is essential; otherwise, we are never going to be competitive in the world of the green future."

The balance between urban and suburban life is a constant tension for local government. "Core urban areas are coming back, even in smaller communities," says Larry Beasley. "That's because a whole generation slowly came to believe in [core renewal]. We built new ideas, we went through the public process involving thousands of people, and we changed those places. That's what this generation is going to have to do with suburbs."

Design elements are relevant in both suburban and urban redevelopment. Protecting and supporting the character of a neighbourhood is important. Cities are getting smarter about how buildings connect and interface with the sidewalk. There are stiffer demands about how the building will "fit" with the community so it doesn't overwhelm a street, and how its landscaping will enhance the greening of that area.

Often, new developments are rising in older suburbs or fringe core properties and these are increasingly mixed-use. How the retail sector is conceived is important to support more street activity: Are bars or coffee shops allowed to leak out onto the sidewalk? How will foot traffic be encouraged? Is there access to public transit? Revitalizing suburban neighbourhoods through retail, commercial, and housing complexes is a strategy that helps the vitality of a community.

Achieving that balance will require forward thinking and offering consumers clear options. "Diversify the choices," adds Larry Beasley. "What we said to the Canadian public is choose the urban model of high-density/high-rise, or choose the suburban model, which is the lowest of the low densities. We haven't offered much else. We have to start offering other things."

Suburbs are varied, one from another. There are common traits, however, and density is one of the most fundamental issues that is coming back to bite planners in the butt.

## Paying for Growth

Suburban sprawl and density issues are the never-ending bane of a planner's existence. Who pays for that growth is the difficult question nagging municipal treasurers and taxpayers.

Jack Diamond has spent much of his professional life looking at these concerns, and believes sprawl is unaffordable from a public policy standpoint.

"For every dollar you get in tax, it costs you $1.40 to service. We have subsidized developers because they don't pay the incremental costs (for subways and expressways). That's what created the suburbs. It has provided complete subservience to the automobile. The provincial governments are the ones that [have allowed this]. We don't have planning; what determines our subways are the sewer systems. If you look at the trunk lines and highways, that's where we have development."

This dilemma is being studied across Canada. Calgary found it could save $11B in future capital costs by adopting a denser growth plan that used 25 percent less land. Halifax Regional Municipality estimated a $700M saving over the next 25 years by increasing its urban density; it already had fully serviced land in its core that could be used for higher density developments. Edmonton estimated that it will have to spend $4B (i.e., expenses exceeding revenue) to service and maintain the infrastructure needs for a number of new planned developments. Several cities in Ontario are significantly increasing their development charges. Cities in other jurisdictions that traditionally haven't charged such fees are now beginning to look at them. Municipalities are starved for dollars.

"The answer to this is full-cost pricing. If every house had to pay its share of the capital investment in the public infrastructure, you'd have a very different outcome," concludes Jack Diamond.

The problem for municipalities is that almost all of the money for servicing is front-end loaded using public dollars – either from annual property taxes or, more likely, through long-term debt, which increases interest payments that must be added to the annual operating budget. Repayments to the municipality occur when the land is bought by developers, building occurs, and homes are eventually sold; but, the municipality is financing the costs and it can take decades to recoup the original investment.

More upfront financing from developers is becoming a preferred solution. Private-public partnerships to develop land are increasing, especially for housing developments. In non-metro areas, it is often difficult to get the private sector to develop industrial land "on spec," which means the municipality becomes responsible for acquiring, servicing, and ultimately selling the land in industrial parks, which are almost always in suburban districts. This need to finance millions of dollars upfront means further pressure on stretched municipal coffers.

## Solutions for Our Suburbs

Increasing suburban density through low- and medium-rise scale is an attractive option for municipalities. In his speech to the 2012 Diamond-Schmitt Urban Futures Lecture, Larry Beasley outlined several steps to help cities improve suburban design:

"First, we can learn a lot from the prevailing scale: more housing, definitely, but maintaining the one-to-three storey building heights, as well as the fine-grained, smaller building pattern. As much as I personally love the striking architecture of towers and the geometry of big building ensembles, and feel they make a lot of sense in downtown areas, transit-oriented developments, and along arterial routes, I think most people feel 'small' is simply better for the suburbs.

"Second, the concept of incremental additions over time – very delicate densification – makes a lot of sense, so putting a lot of options for change within the zoning of a new suburban subdivision allows that community to evolve in a natural way. Planners call this "invisible density" or "hidden density." You start with a slightly higher density than we generally see in subdivisions because lot sizes and street space are smaller, but you add more as you go along, achieving the 30 to 40 units per acre target in a painless way. Recent subdivisions usually start at about six to 10 units per acre, so it is not a big jump to get to the densities we need.

"Third, we can learn a lot from the diversity that you see in the old neighbourhoods: all kinds of households; many lot and house sizes and types (single family homes, but also duplexes, back lane units, apartments over shops, home conversions, infill housing); and many architectural styles; a rich socio-economic range, from low-income to quite wealthy households; a lot of independent retail potential, rather than just 'big boxes'; and many workplace and live/work possibilities. This diversity opens up economic opportunity close by, as well as providing a plausible framework for a wide social engagement and supportive community life.

"Fourth, there are so many benefits of the local commercial 'high street' model, with building fronts proud to the sidewalk, parking lots behind, shops with offices and apartments above. This can also be a good template for conversion of the existing malls and that strip retail that sits within a sea of parking. This is the 'placemaking' form that engenders localized uniqueness and really sticks in the memory, but is also the realm for sustained social relations and interchange. It offers economic potential for start-up operations, and fosters walking.

"Fifth, narrower streets and back lanes can be a big bonus. The traditional lane-and-a-half driving area for a residential street naturally calms traffic, is safer for children at play, and takes up less land. Back lanes offer utility access and trash handling without compromising the streetscape, and cut the number of vehicle crossings over the sidewalk. The lanes actually give the "front door" primacy to the façade of a house, rather than that ever-present 'garage door' image.

"Sixth, whether you see curvy streets or a straight grid pattern, the connectivity of the whole system, especially for pedestrians, is beneficial. Many planners don't like cul-de-sacs, but it seems a lot of consumers do – so what is important is that they not be designed as pedestrian dead-ends, but include walking linkages ... that's what you often see in the old neighbourhoods.

"Seventh, you will find the old neighbourhoods always work well for transit and the levels of ridership usually make transit viable without much subsidy. This means people can own fewer cars and spend less for their mobility (but this is not about getting rid of cars – it's about offering other options for many of the trips that don't need to be done in a car); people are also less victimized by gas price fluctuations; and more people in the household can get around more independently.

"And lastly, that whole emphasis on landscape and gardening in the traditional neighbourhoods is really important to bring back to future suburban planning, rather than have landscape be such a secondary consideration with new subdivisions. Nothing gives a place a more gracious, homey feel than a nice row of street trees. Nothing is friendlier than an attractive front flower garden, unique to each house and tended by the residents. Nothing helps local food sourcing more than an individual vegetable garden. We don't need wide front yards or extra-large lots to make these things happen – we simply need more motivation to use landscaping strategically and keep it up over the long run."

Larry Beasley's thoughtful comments show that there are solutions for the suburban dilemma. Lots of people like living in the suburbs. It is up to municipalities to develop innovative ideas on how to change the traditional planning and design of suburbs, pay for the infrastructure, and ensure the quality of life for families is sustainable.

The sustainability and use of land is a fundamental question for councils to consider more carefully in the future. There are consequences for converting agricultural land or natural spaces to housing or commercial development.

"We are diminishing our agricultural and recreational land to a very marked degree. That's another very serious long-term issue that includes our food supply and contaminating our water supply. In the short term, it's not affordable; in the long term, it's a disaster," says Jack Diamond.

Remaking and refocusing suburban life and lifestyles will be one of the great challenges in the years ahead for urban planners,

architects, and land use experts. It touches on critical issues such
as a municipality's financial capacity, public transit, infrastructure
priorities, urban design, live-where-you-work trends, local health,
our car-centric society, greening our communities, and the evolving
need for different housing options that will accommodate our much
more diverse family units.

Suburban life accommodates many Canadian families. Two issues
have emerged: first, the future for our existing suburbs and how
they are redesigned; and second, how new suburbs will be financed,
designed, and operated. There is growing consensus that we need
a new model; the traditional method is not sustainable. This is the
challenge for municipal planners in the rest of the 21st century.

Part of the answer will be how we adapt to continued leaps in technology. The millennial generation lives and works on tablets and
other portable devices. That is already impacting traditional office
towers and how companies and governments have done business.
Technology advances and global linkages will continue to change
how we work and where we live.

Part of the answer will also be found in the new urban lifestyle, and
how people are going to afford housing in the future.

# CHAPTER 9

# THE URBAN EXPERIENCE

*"Nobody goes there anymore. It's too crowded."* – *Yogi Berra*

Hard work, innovative thinking, and many, many billions of dollars have helped to reshape urban landscapes in the past 25 years.

For a lot of large and small communities around the world, urban life has improved. There are more feet on the street. There is more energy downtown. Most urban cores are safer than in years prior. There have been conscientious efforts to make buildings and spaces greener, often with considerable success. Public art has become more interesting. The quality of daily life on the street has gotten better. Design has ripened as urban planners and architects creatively seek new opportunities and repurpose older buildings. Many municipalities have invested significantly in improving their downtowns and attracting more people to live in the core.

Rightly or wrongly, a lot of people still judge a community by the vibrancy and vigour of its downtown. If people are bustling, businesses are prospering, streets are clean, and there is electricity in the air, people instinctively believe that the community itself is progressive and successful.

Municipalities are learning that many critical aspects compose their public image, many of which can be controlled or influenced by a smart community. As we move deeper into the 21st century, local governments are awakening to important new factors that support great urban cores.

## Animating Public Places and Spaces

European cities have understood for decades the importance of designing and programming public places and spaces. European families usually reside in very compact spaces, resulting in high urban density. Often, they don't have lavish private homes. As a result, they tend to live and socialize in the public realm.

North American cities have been much slower to embrace that concept. However, with ever-smaller condos and apartments, and the growing movement towards urban life, that reality is impinging on our communities more and more.

Public places and spaces are where people connect; where they do business in markets and stores; where a strong social environment is encouraged. Urban spaces are where people enjoy much of their leisure time and experiences.

Stockholm has beautifully-designed places in and around the core. They also program them, offering entertainment, buskers, events, and street food. These features keep the quality and freshness of the experience to a high standard. The city has cleverly designed streets and squares for public use – providing easy access to electrical outlets, using natural amphitheatres, and designing their network of streets so some can be closed to easily become larger public spaces.

Amsterdam designs its transportation system to encourage cyclists, pedestrians, and families to use public places and spaces. Paris pays buskers to play and entertain in subway stops and other public places.

Civic programming of public spaces is richly alive in these cities, says Larry Beasley. He also notes one other critical element of success: "They have regulatory freedom for private activity on the edges of public spaces – for example, restaurants and coffee shops that spill out into public spaces. We have many rules that limit that in North America," he concludes ruefully.

The café society of Italy, Spain, and other countries is typical of that combination of the public and private realms. That is why cars are limited on piazzas and public squares in European and South American cities. Human interaction takes precedence.

Municipalities in North America don't yet fully understand the importance of animating and supporting their public spaces. We have too many bleak, cold, unused spaces that people simply rush through instead of enjoying. There is no connectivity.

Local governments need to become collaborators with the private sector. They need to budget a bit of money for programming events and activities. They need to design public places and spaces better, so they can be adapted for spontaneous public use.

"Lots of cities make the mistake of trying to be, or trying to replicate, successes from elsewhere. That doesn't work. Melbourne has tried to be ourselves, and that's partly the architecture, partly the public spaces ... we're very interested in the public realm," says Lord Mayor Robert Doyle.

"There are competitive advantages to improving the quality of the public realm," agrees Larry Beasley. "They must be maintained. You can't just leave gashes of asphalt all over town."

Elected people need to become better attuned to public needs. There is often insensitivity to the public realm and its importance to residents and visitors. Too often, people walk or drive through a city and never engage with it. That engagement starts with a lively experience and enjoyment of the public places and spaces.

## Bringing New Life to Old Public Buildings

In many neighbourhoods, the school and the church were historically the centre of community life.

Today, as our demographics shift dramatically and we become a much more cosmopolitan society, many of these anchor institutions are being closed. This can have a devastating impact on neighbourhoods. The impact may be particularly dramatic for small towns, who see their character being changed as their population hollows-out.

There are three key signs for declining neighbourhoods: schools, churches, and shops. When they begin to falter, it almost always follows that people begin leaving or selling their homes (or, in worst cases, abandoning them).

*Schools* – Parents want modern schools in better districts to ensure their kids get a head-start. School boards are abandoning older schools with declining populations. This scenario is sometimes compounded by a growing social concern – income inequality and school results. There is some evidence that wealth and school test scores are connected; wealthier neighbourhoods are often producing higher student results than schools in poorer areas.

*Churches* – Second, as society ages and new denominations appear in large suburban churches, attendance in traditional neighbourhood places of worship is declining. Parishes can't afford to keep up the property and pay staff. A church closing is very significant for that neighbourhood.

*Shops* – Finally, traditional shops and stores are closing because of a lack of business. As the town or neighbourhood undergoes transformation, mom-and-pop stores are often a casualty. This also impacts the character of the town or neighbourhood, and how the street is perceived.

Cities are now trying to spur redevelopment of such properties. There are a number of options being tried. Usually, the neighbourhood has a prominent view on redevelopment, and conflict is not unusual. Successful projects require honest community engagement, sensitivity to local concerns and heritage, innovative ideas, and substantial capital investments.

Some ideas emerging include the following.

*New living space* – Condos or apartments can be created from old schools or churches. Often, the bones of the building are appealing, and there is usually ample parking and green space around the site; shadowing is not an issue because the building's outside is not being changed dramatically. Adding new residents back into the neighbourhood is a great benefit. This also gets the property onto the tax rolls.

*Creative space* – Artscape opened "Artscape Youngplace" in 2013. They bought an abandoned school in west Toronto and renovated it into a new community cultural hub and home for artists, galleries, and a children's centre. Artists can own their own studios, which helps them build equity and stability.

*Entertainment space* – Depending on location and proximity to homes, sometimes these buildings can provide attractive renovation opportunities to potential house restaurants or other entertainment-oriented businesses. An auditorium in an old school, for example, might be adapted for a comedy club, little theatre, or other entertainment purposes.

*Business space* – A wide variety of alternative business purposes can be developed, such as labs for science and research; "hotelling" business space (that is, temporary use of desks and technology by business people who are on the road a lot and don't need expansive office facilities); concierge office facilities, where companies rent an office and share a receptionist/board room; etc.

*Community space* – Often, the local neighbourhood has considerable attachment to the school or church, and will fight to either keep it open or to have the municipality take it over and keep it in the public domain. This can be problematic for councils, as they are reluctant to make a precedent for one neighbourhood, and then deny another one. But, repurposing such a facility as a senior's centre, community centre, child-care facility, etc. is often a useful idea for a city. The old gym can become a new health and fitness centre.

*Local food emporium* – With the growing interest in local food, a creative concept involving community garden plots, wood-fired bake ovens, food and craft outlets, farmers' market, community café, and other food-related ideas can be a delicious alternative to this otherwise dead space.

*Health centre* – Convert the school or church into a community health care centre. Offer rehab services. Provide safe child care. Create a fitness centre for kids and families. Teach English as a Second Language courses. Work with immigrant families on assimilating into the neighbourhood. Provide health information and care.

*Affordable housing* – Working with Habitat for Humanity and social agencies, older facilities can be transformed into affordable housing for seniors, low-income families, or people with disabilities.

*High-tech centre* – Start-up companies and young entrepreneurs are always looking for interesting, cheap communal space in which to work. They love a collaborative environment where ideas can be flung around. A school provides an interesting concept for creating this communal open space, and repurposed classrooms are ideal for individual company activities.

*Social enterprise centre* – There is an interest in having social agencies and community organizations share space. Advantages are access to board rooms, AV facilities, and so on – without having each agency spend its own dollars on rarely-used facilities. These organizations also often discover collaborative opportunities and end up working together.

## Public Art

"The Cloud Gate" is a giant metal sculpture that adorns Chicago's Millennium Park. It is adored by residents and visitors alike, it has been a backdrop for movie scenes and countless photographs, and it helps to create a glorious atmosphere for the city's waterfront.

That's the potency of a great piece of public art. It speaks to and about a city. It sets a tone and merrily shouts about the community's vision and commitment to creativity and culture.

Public art should engage you. There should be an emotional response: laughter, contemplation, amusement, provocation, even indignation or pique.

There is growing appreciation in municipal circles about the value and importance of public art, but we have a long way to go.

Some cities have adopted the "one percent policy," in which they allocate an additional one percent of the capital cost of major above-ground projects to a reserve fund. It is used to support superior design elements, to enhance landscaping and lighting, or for creating, installing, and maintaining (and sometimes even decommissioning) public art. In other words, it is dedicated to enhancing the public realm. The fund can also be augmented by the public benefits that developers are required to contribute so they can obtain density bonusing (getting a couple of additional floors in a high rise, for example). Private donors can also bequeath dollars to support public art.

Public art can be controversial, which is why I believe strongly that politicians should be kept well away from the decision-making process. The idea of untrained elected officials having a public debate about whether or not a piece of public art should be installed is horrifying. An independent peer-review panel offers a much better process, perhaps under the auspices of the local arts council.

Municipalities need to be sure they don't regulate the life out of public art. City councils need to help with financing, set parameters, then get out of the way.

Public art offers both a social and an economic benefit to communities. It stirs passion and can create a gathering point for wildly diverse people. It is important for public art not to stagnate or become complacent, and it must push boundaries.

The critical point is whether or not the community is going to embrace this cultural advancement. It is a big, long-term commitment. Cities like Montreal, Chicago, Paris, Melbourne, Rome, and others have made this a community priority. They force innovative thinking and design. They demand cutting-edge art. They support creativity in all its forms.

From a popular sculpture garden to wondrous vistas in a park, from gallant murals on building walls to an iconic water feature in the downtown, from a dazzling light show projected onto the walls of city hall to an impromptu event on a street corner, public art in all of its many forms adds life and energy to a city.

Public art doesn't have to be static – it can move, surprise, and shock. In Tokyo, Japan and London, England, public art went underground – to the subways. Using digital media, large screens, and giant billboards, unique artistic forms and expressions are displayed on subway walls and entrances.

Smart communities now understand that special vibe that helps to attract interesting people who want to live, work, and create jobs in exciting, fun cities.

Municipalities need to do a much better job of persuading philanthropists to invest in our cities and towns. Sometimes, public art is an entrée to a larger contribution from philanthropists.

Public art should be a celebration. It should create a vibrant discussion about how art and architecture can happily collide, and what the result says about the character of that city. Art should raise the civility of a city. It should elevate our spirit and emotions. It may even spark a new arts district in a community, with all of the benefits that can bring.

Public art is free. It is accessible. It makes a statement about that community and its vision. We have undervalued public art in our society. That needs to change. And, municipalities are the ones that have to lead.

## New Life for Little Spaces

If you took an aerial photograph of any city, you would discover interesting little nooks and crannies that have been forgotten or ignored. They come in many shapes and sizes – an unused lot, a small space that has become overgrown, an abandoned gas station on a corner, an odd little triangle between buildings, a pathway ...

A smart community will recognize that opportunity to repurpose these little connectors, these pieces of urban life that have been bypassed. With very modest investments, such a space can often become a little gem or a green oasis in a concrete jungle. A bit of landscaping, a park bench, some swings for kids, a piece of interesting art, a quiet corner where people can socialize or simply contemplate ...

Rediscovering these spaces is a fun part of a community's effort to support connectivity. Sometimes, community groups will take responsibility for the project, or a local corporation will make it part of their charitable work. Reclaimed green space helps to civilize a sometimes uncivilized world, and offers a bit of peace and comfort to citizens who are often buried under daily pressures.

This is also a way to make a city or downtown or neighbourhood more walkable, livelier, and more appealing. As John Nicholson says, "Public space helps to define a city. It is shared. There is a risk today of the community being absent, of social media replacing walking and talking together. People need this social interaction."

These revitalized spaces have a positive effect on a community. Many young people are becoming more engaged with the design and possibilities of what that space might be.

Each time the municipality touches the public realm is an opportunity to improve it. For example, if a municipality digs up a street for sewer work, it should be contemplating what that street will look like after. It gives new chances to refresh and refurbish, and the neighbourhood should be engaged in that improvement process. That step is sometimes absent.

"Local leadership is critical," says John Nicholson. "You have to get to a decision, and then execute it. You can't just paint pretty pictures, you need to get it done. Then you need to protect it. Absent strong leadership, it all flounders."

## Land Banks

If you don't own the land, you're not much of a player in the game. That is a hard reality that municipalities must understand.

Very few cities have comprehensive programs for land-banking any more. In fact, most municipalities own a surprisingly small amount of land (excluding parks and natural places that are in the public domain).

City manager Jeff Fielding believes that "Cities need to land bank. [Too many cities] have no vision. People need to understand that these are legacies for future generations."

When a city controls land, it can use it for public projects, or land swaps with developers to encourage new development that will expand the tax base. A progressive city can use it to revitalize an entire downtown, as Saskatoon did in the 1960s when it persuaded the railroad to move out of its downtown. That sparked a significant downtown renaissance.

Collectively, public institutions own/control a considerable amount of land, including schools, college campuses, federal and provincial government buildings and lands, natural areas controlled by conservation authorities, hospitals and health care facilities, and recreation areas.

There has been a noticeable lack of cooperation between and amongst public stewards of urban lands. That relationship has to be rethought. Part of the problem is that the various orders of government and public bodies seem to have forgotten that it is taxpayer money that has already paid for the land and any buildings on it – and there is only one taxpayer.

So, today we have the bizarre situation in which various public bodies may be fighting with each other, charging another public organization "market rates" for public property, and usually tying-up properties for many years in bureaucratic nonsense and indifference, while lands and buildings sit vacant and under-developed.

Surely there is a better way to coordinate, plan, develop, bank, and use land for public betterment.

## Brownfield Sites and Vacant Lands

Brownfield properties are one of the greatest challenges and most important opportunities for urban renewal and redevelopment. Chronically vacant properties are another. Communities have come up with some solutions, but are limited by legislation that varies by province.

Brownfields can range from unsightly old factories with land so corrupted that nobody will touch the property, to abandoned gas stations on city street corners, to crumbling houses that are collapsing from neglect (and sometimes the deliberate indifference of the owner).

Municipalities are terribly vulnerable to brownfield issues. People hate the sight of a dirty, broken property that deteriorates by the day. At the same time, many municipalities are reluctant to take over such properties, even in a tax sale, because the local government then takes on the environmental responsibility – and that can mean millions, even tens of millions, in costs and potential liabilities.

There has been some easing of legal responsibilities if a municipality assumes a brownfield site, and a greater effort to hold previous owners accountable for these properties. Still, it can be a political and financial minefield for councils.

Some municipalities are now advancing a community improvement plan to resolve brownfield sites. By identifying contaminated sites, they can develop a strategy, which will often include some tax relief/incentive programs.

A tax increment grant (sometimes in partnership with other orders of government) is another tool to encourage clean-up of contaminated sites. It can offer financial assistance to the private sector to help offset the costs of remediation of brownfield sites. The objective is to remove the contaminants so the environment is improved and the property can be repurposed.

Land that has been vacant for some time is another issue. Municipal enterprise zones are sometimes created to support the revitalization of a particular block or neighbourhood. This often allows governments to provide incentive programs and special funding to developers who propose affordable housing, for example, or mixed-use developments.

Incentives might include tax rebates; tax cancellation or forgiveness for a specified number of years; grants for remediation studies; financial assistance for remediation of the site; and redevelopment grants to help meet specific local needs for that site.

What is not productive is for municipalities to simply turn a blind eye to the problem. They need to identify and prioritize site remediation. They need to work with owners on innovative local solutions to salvage these sites. They need to be tougher with recalcitrant owners. They need to step up and develop answers with the other orders of government. They need to support partnerships with incentives and opportunities. They need to bring life back to dead brownfield sites and chronically vacant properties.

## Waterfronts

We have always been seduced by the charms of water.

Most great cities have a direct connection with water. That history is based upon pure necessity – people need water to survive. Waterways provide transportation corridors, food, waste disposal, recreation, and other benefits. Whether it is a lake, river, ocean, or harbour, water has helped to shape and form many communities. We really like waterfronts and living near water.

What is fascinating is that, even in the 21st century, some communities have turned their backs on this amazing resource. Progressive communities have embraced it, however, and developed a close relationship.

Chicago and Toronto are often compared; most observers would agree that Chicago has done an exemplary job of connecting with Lake Michigan and developing a great people-oriented public space. Toronto has spent decades in talk, inaction, and wildly inappropriate ideas. The city has substantially blocked the view of Lake Ontario with a wall of condos as people drive in from the west. Only in recent years has planning and action begun to better celebrate and make use of Toronto's waterfront.

Sydney, Helsinki, and San Francisco are just some of many smart cities that have embraced their waterfront district. Wonderful heritage properties are being repurposed as restaurants, clubs, bars, and tourist attractions. These districts quickly become favorites.

"In Melbourne, the biggest challenge we face is $5B of development around the docklands," says Robert Doyle. It is a remarkable opportunity to develop new residential and commercial space around their waterfront – 600 hectares, of which only half is developed. "Over the next 30 years, all of that will be urban renewal. If we don't get that right, that will destroy the livability of the city because the footprint of the central city will expand," he concludes.

Stockholm, really a city of islands, has made water its focus. It has set aside 40 percent of its land for green space and waterfront public access. Rio de Janeiro's gorgeous beachfront (where Copacabana and Ipanema *do* exist – and are legendary) sets the social and cultural tone for that entire city.

Shanghai is unique – it has both river and sea exposure. The huge international port is a significant driver of the local economy, and is now the busiest container port in the world. The Bund Riverwalk attracts thousands of people enjoying old-European buildings and very modern Asian skyscrapers on both sides of the river.

San Antonio's River Walk has been carefully nurtured by the city for decades. It is now an immense tourist attraction offering food, arts and crafts, entertainment, and accommodations to five million visitors annually. It generates an $8B annual economic impact. Hotels and bars abut the water, barges glide down the river, and each bridge is specially designed. This focal point for the city includes a convention centre that straddles the river, and lovely paths for people to stroll, nibble, and enjoy live entertainment and many festivals and events.

Venice is defined by its waterways. While the city is facing serious environmental issues, the waterways are really the streets of Venice, leading to great piazzas and public gathering spaces. This availability of social meeting places is one of the keys to developing great waterfronts. Accessibility is another critical element.

Canadian cities often haven't done a very good job of interfacing with a river or water, notes architect John Nicholson. This connection to nature, however, provides great opportunities.

"The greatest attraction is a natural setting," says Jeff Fielding. "People appreciate having that kind of space available. We need lots of political courage. We need great vision and to make the investments."

In Canada, port cities like Victoria, Montreal, Charlottetown, Nanaimo, Halifax, and others have done great work in developing and enhancing their waterfront as people-oriented gathering places. Saskatoon has developed a terrific park/pathway along its river. Winnipeg opened the Esplanade Riel with a restaurant in the middle of the pedestrian bridge. Cities are finally getting smarter about connecting with their waterfronts.

Restaurants, clubs, and bars provide a social base, and lively music and public art adorn waterfronts. People have a natural affinity for

water, and a smartly-developed harbour or riverwalk quickly becomes a focal point for the community and an attraction for visitors.

Great waterfronts have a number of similarities. There is usually a
grand promenade along the water to encourage walking and family
fun. Cars are restricted. There is a lively social atmosphere, with
food, fun, music, performers, entertainers, and lots of action. The
natural setting of the harbour or waterfront is enhanced, not overly-
developed, to allow the beauty and ambience of nature to shine.
Heritage properties are respected and salvaged. Great spectacles are
often presented, including fireworks, water competitions, regattas,
and more.

Water has a calming influence on most people. The differences
between a waterfront and a bustling downtown street, often just a
block or two away, can be striking. Waterfronts can provide a calm,
peaceful oasis in an often frantic world.

Many great cities have been formed around their harbour, river, or
waterfront. Those cities lucky enough to have this natural attraction
are blessed. The issue is whether or not the local council has the
wisdom and creativity to preserve, enhance, and support this marvellous gift from nature.

## Transformative Projects

On a rare occasion, communities may have the opportunity to in-
dulge in a huge, transformative project.

Sometimes, it is a tragic fire that wipes out a block or two of a
downtown. Or a tornado or hurricane that in mere seconds destroys
a community that took a hundred years to build (as happened to
Goderich, Ontario in 2011). Or another catastrophe such as the ter-
rorist attack that struck New York City on 9/11 and forever changed
its skyline. Or the earthquake that shook Christchurch, New Zealand.

How a community – and how its mayor and council – respond to a
calamity speaks to the character of that community. Almost always,
out of that tragedy comes an opportunity for renewal and a coming-
together of the community.

Then, there are the deliberate decisions to re-energize a city. Perhaps the most recent significant transformation was "The Big Dig" in Boston. The $15B project (which, predictably, went massively over budget) buried 5.6 kilometres of a raised highway that ran through the city. In its place, a series of small parks were created on the "roof" of the buried highway. The concept was to modify and rebuild city blocks around the road project, redirecting traffic flows through Boston and changing the tenor of the streets. This mega-project was one of those "once in a lifetime" initiatives.

In Medellin, Columbia, several years of urban renewal projects have helped the metamorphosis of this once dangerous city into a modern, progressive community. The multi-faceted projects included an elevated gondola tramway that connected some of the community's poorest districts to the city; new libraries, schools, parks, and science centres built in impoverished neighbourhoods; and ambitious public works programs to transform this once deadly city into a thriving urban hub.

"From the beginning, we involved the people in the activity of using public spaces to solve social problems and to change the lives of the community," said then-director of Urban Works Alejandro Echeverri. The solution was to build the most beautiful buildings in the poorest areas of the city.

To accomplish such a transformation takes inordinate vision and courage. And money. The investment will be massive, and partnerships of all orders of government, the private sector, and philanthropists will be required.

Big change demands big vision. That's where the process fails for most communities today.

"We need political courage," says Jeff Fielding. "We've become very much status quo. Everybody's afraid of taking a risk and not being successful. We need great vision, and to make great investments."

The city hall veteran acknowledges another critical point about today's municipal climate: "You can't make a mistake [as a bureaucrat]. If we are going to be creative, there's a chance of making a mistake, but everybody is so careful, so tight ... we won't take risks anymore."

It is a telling statement. That negative, self-protective vibe that many politicians exude discourages managers, or even community leaders, from proposing really bold and innovative ideas and projects. Too often, there are negative political attacks and reactions before there is even a legitimate debate about a proposal.

Bureaucrats and politicians both very quickly decide: Why take a chance? Why expose myself to attacks in the media? Why cause a storm of controversy about an idea? Why make a big proposal to transform a block or promote a project, knowing that I'll become exposed and vulnerable to the angry political process?

For many inside city hall, it just isn't worth it. For administrators, politicians too often attack them publicly, giving them little chance to respond or defend themselves. For politicians, there will always be negative media response or attacks from political enemies. It truly does take courage to propose a major project or idea, because many people simply don't like change or can't envisage a project of great magnitude.

As Eddie Friel says bluntly, "The public sector can get into such a dysfunctional state that trying to get anything done [becomes] impossible, and trying to do the right thing is considered insanity."

With the bitterness and negativity of the political process today, it becomes increasingly difficult for projects to be advanced. Our communities are poorer for that. The extremists on both sides of the political process seem to be more concerned about the shouting on tonight's news clip than the future of their community.

Municipalities need to rise above the pettiness of local politics and the nastiness of national politics. We can build great communities and transform broken neighbourhoods, but not without extraordinary leadership, strong commitment, and courage.

There are great communities in the world. We need to learn from them, and demand more of our political leaders.

# CHAPTER 10

# INTRIGUING, ENGAGING CITIES

*"A city is the pulsating product of the human hand and mind, reflecting man's history, his struggle for freedom, creativity, genius – and his selfishness and errors."* – Charles Abram

Cities and towns should invoke our passion, our civic patriotism, and a love for our community that is never quite forgotten.

There is a vibe to a good city, a feeling you get. Perhaps no one can fully explain it, but most of us have experienced it – you get energized, enthused, excited. Sometimes, you are mesmerized by the beauty and appeal of the city, its people, and its aura. Its natural environment. Some cities exude an intensity and fervor that inspire and attract. Some inveigle us to try things we wouldn't risk in our hometown.

Sometimes, though, you get wary, fearful, and nervous in a community. It somehow gives off a negative vibe. Sometimes, you are simply repulsed and never go back. If a city doesn't arouse us, if we are bored and apathetic, if it doesn't appeal to our spirit, then we are likely to respond by ignoring it.

Cities should move us, touch us, with many varied emotions. We should feel things about cities. That's one of the magnificent realities of why we love and hate cities, and why we are so fascinated by them.

As Jane Jacobs observed in *The Death and Life of Great American Cities*, "Dull, inert cities contain the seeds of their own destruction and little else. But lively, diverse, intense cities contain the seeds of their own regeneration, with energy enough to carry over for problems and needs outside themselves."

The physical design and layout of a city is a crucial building block: how a city uses its public realm and its natural assets; how it respects and protects its heritage; how it understands the importance of social opportunity in its public spaces; how citizens are engaged.

Discussed below are some cities of the world that are particularly intriguing, cities that have accomplished or overcome some local government challenge, and from which we can learn something about urban life. There is no order or ranking, just things to contemplate or admire as we explore fascinating cities around the world.

## Hong Kong, Vancouver, New York City

What do they share? They are all "island cities" – that is, they are pretty much surrounded by water. That means land has always been at a premium, so they have all developed a simple formula: build up, not out.

In today's environment, that has turned out to be a really good model for sustainable urban development. Forced to avoid sprawl, these cities developed a density and a vibrant urban core that many cities in the world today seek.

That density has meant a diverse, cosmopolitan, and vibrant lifestyle. Space is at a premium, so nooks and crannies are used by somebody, for something. Foods from around the world to feed the many cultures, fascinating little districts and markets, and bustling streets are common themes.

Vehicles are costly to operate and park, so private automobiles are not predominant. As a result, public transportation is a critical issue. It must be reliable and relatively inexpensive. The airport transportation in Hong Kong is the best I've experienced: you can take your luggage to the downtown train terminal, check in with the airline and leave your bags, then walk downtown to visit your tailor or have a meal, then catch the high-speed train to the airport, where you stroll through security, and a few hours later pick up your luggage in Bangkok or your final destination.

These cities have learned the importance of public transportation to move large numbers of people safely and quickly. They have clearly understood the issue of density because of the physical limitations of their geography. City planners need to move people and traffic, and that can be a considerable challenge. Bridges can quickly become choke-points for traffic flows.

They have created really dynamic cities that attract bright minds, the creative sector, and smart entrepreneurs. Their economies are diverse, they are technologically advanced, and they have a terrific vitality of life and local culture.

These cities have utilized their waterfronts effectively. Hong Kong's harbour is the site of great spectacles and public events. New York has the iconic Statue of Liberty and other public art to celebrate its waterfront. Vancouver has done a wonderful job of developing its Sea Wall as a great open space, and encouraging private developers to include water features in their buildings and the public/private spaces around them. Views of harbours are highly prized by residential developers – and big premiums are paid for a great view.

The compactness of urban life has forced these three cities to run civic services efficiently. They all cherish public spaces. They aggressively seek green spaces for families to enjoy. There is a street presence radiating from buildings; many buildings are retail on the ground floor, commercial for several floors above, and then living space higher up. High-rise complexes are usually designed with setbacks to make them more compatible with the street. Care is taken to interface the building with the sidewalk.

The downside of these cities is cost. Housing prices are very high and seemingly going ever-higher. Because of the cost to develop floor space, living space is getting smaller. That means public places and spaces become ever more important.

Each city has chosen to animate itself in different ways. In New York and Hong Kong, buildings are bright at night with brilliantly-lit, colourful animated displays criss-crossing office towers and huge electronic signs shouting their wares. Vancouver is more laid back, with an emphasis on the sea, sky, and mountains that are only a few miles away, with all of the recreational opportunities they afford.

All of these cities have a strong commitment to cultural activities and expression. The arts in all forms are celebrated. The very diverse communities mean a throbbing cultural diaspora. They are very fashion conscious. New media are highly visible. Young artists, performers, and entertainers come to take a chance on developing their careers.

Business is important. Making money is celebrated. Entrepreneurs and the bold are encouraged. There is a youthful energy to these cities that makes them highly appealing to graduates choosing where to live.

*The Takeaway: Great cities need high density. They need energy and street activity. They need the vibe and buzz of youth. They support vigorous cultural and commercial activity.*

## From Portland to Portland

What came first, the culture or the community? Nature versus nurture – does that apply to cities?

In other words, what impact has place had on the development of the local culture/business climate/attitude of its people? How has that translated into the city of today? Is the city now a reflection of the people and its geography?

Portland, Maine and Portland, Oregon are interesting case studies. Located on opposite sides of the United States and facing different oceans, the two cities are vastly different, yet have some interesting similarities.

Portland, Maine is a gritty, hard-working city that has survived a lot of economic ups and downs. It is located in a state known for its taciturn and somewhat stoic people. It has survived and been hardened by four devastating fires since its founding in the early 1600s, a rough climate, and the roller-coaster of a natural resources-based economy.

The city has done a fabulous job of reinventing its downtown and forging a new connection to the local harbour. It is a historic seacoast town with a working waterfront. That makes it a distinctive and appealing tourist destination – and the harbour district is the starting point for visitors.

Tourists stroll the streets and wharves, wandering in and out of fishmongers and restaurants featuring the catch of the day, as you watch the boat that caught the fish bobbing at anchor. Refurbished heritage buildings are attractive retail outlets, often for artists and artisans who offer unique creations. Museums and galleries abound.

What is particularly relevant is that a downtown mall built in the 1970s had the usual negative impact on the downtown. It wasn't until the 1990s that the city realized the treasure it had in its waterfront and old port. That new community focus and commitment sparked the revitalization of the city. It came from the local community rallying together to discover its own attributes, and to commit to a new focus and direction.

There is a charm and energy to this city of 66,000. Art walks and guided tours are readily available. The city has survived; in fact, its motto is "I will rise again." It has. And, having overcome natural and man-made civic disasters, today is a thriving New England city.

Named after its Maine counterpart, Portland, Oregon has become renowned for its strong neighbourhoods, for its commitment to green energy and policies, and as a resilient place for people to live and grow.

The city is number one in the U.S. for library circulation rates. It has long championed local food, and its unique food trucks offer wonderful streetside dining. The city supports local arts and artists, neighbourhood shops, a strong educational strategy, and being a healthy city. It is culturally active.

Because of careful land use planning, Portland has a reputation as one of the greenest cities in the world. It has imposed an urban growth boundary that restricts suburban sprawl and has provided protection for agricultural lands. It has an award-winning mass transportation system that includes light rail and streetcars. The city has turned some intersections into urban piazzas, which helps to slow traffic and promote a neighbourhood feel. Some residents have even put couches on a street corner, just to share the urban experience.

Residents pride themselves on the parks and natural spaces through-out the community, highlighted by an entwined series of protected urban parks. Neighbourhoods and home owners make concerted efforts to support a green city and residential districts. The city has an aggressive plan for sustainability.

This heritage of environmental responsibility has metamorphosed into a thriving green economy that has made the city one of the world's leading exporters of environmentally-friendly products and services.

The port and shipping facilities have long been an economic driver for the city. The river port leading to the Pacific Ocean is one of the most important in the northwest. Like its counterpart a few thousand miles away, the Rose City has developed an interesting port district that is also a key part of the city's economic vitality.

The city has also become a world-renowned home for sports manu-facturing – Nike, of course, and others – and the strong local com-mitment to fitness and running provided much of the early impetus for this industry. Cycling is a significant part of local transportation planning and the city offers a lovely green pathway that connects parks and public spaces.

*The Takeaway: I have long believed in an analogy that I thought up years ago: imagine a horse-drawn wagon. Council (the driver) holds the reins that guides the wagon (the city), but it is the horses (voters) that provide the locomotion and ultimately decide where it (the city) is going. The people have the power.*

*Both Portlands show the importance of reflecting local residents in the culture, economy, and community. They show that building the economy from a city's heritage, its geographic location, natural re-sources, and the resilience and determination of its people to over-come challenges results in a solid economic base. Exploiting what is distinctive about that city and region makes each city unique and appealing.*

## Beijing

Gather every man, woman, and child in Ontario and Quebec and put them in one city; welcome to Beijing.

The city is currently building its sixth ring road. It has two more on the books. Its airport is likely to soon become the busiest in the world. High-speed trains link several key Chinese cities, and these trains are superb – better than any in North America.

The urbanization of China (and other emerging economies including India, Southeast Asia, Africa, and South America) is one of the great demographic transformations of the 21st century.

The investments in infrastructure have been enormous. Financed primarily by the central government, the infrastructure improvements have propelled the growth of the city. High-rise apartments have shot up across the city and, with them, escalating real estate prices. The price of real estate is a constant theme across Chinese society.

This rapid growth has created problems: traffic is full volume; pollution is a serious problem and air quality is often abysmal; government corruption is endemic; and health and safety standards are not always enforced or observed. Many families were dislocated when their small homes in hutongs (narrow streets or alleys) were taken over to make way for towering residential complexes, often without adequate compensation.

Despite these issues, Beijing today is one of the world's most engaging cities. It throbs with energy. Fabulous food can be found in a thousand restaurants, in markets, and on the streets. Shopping districts pulse with energy most hours of the day and night. Business is booming. Young people are energetic, entrepreneurial, and dedicated; they work hard. Kids go to school and university and study ferociously to achieve great marks.

The city has done a fine job of preserving or reconstructing its many heritage assets, from the Forbidden City to temples and public spaces. Tourists are flocking to visit, often climbing the Great Wall of China, located about an hour north of Beijing.

The Olympic Games opened the city to the world, and the events were wonderfully organized. Innovative architecture is encouraged, from the home of Chinese television (a very unique A-shaped building, towering in black glass) to shapely hotels that feature modern electronic screens five-storeys high on the face of their buildings.

Beijing features many attractive public places and spaces throughout the city. Tranquil parks and waterways, glorious public monuments, immense public spaces like Tiananmen Square, and treasured
heritage sites are found throughout the city. Respect for culture, the
arts, and the work of artisans resonates throughout the city's many
districts.

There is a lot of money floating around Beijing, which abounds with
lavish seven-star hotels and pricey shopping districts. Beijing has a
disproportionate number of people seeking luxury items.

With this new affluence has come a growing divide between
wealthy and poor – something that western societies and other
emerging urban economies are wrestling with as well. The standards
of living are separating. This chasm will become one of the great
societal challenges of the 21st century for many cities and countries.

*The Takeaway: There is some question if Beijing's explosive growth
could have happened without powerful (central) government action
to support the local government – both through expropriation and
from the investment of billions in infrastructure and civic improvements. The central government of China clearly understands the
importance of redeveloping urban centres as the country's economic, social and cultural drivers, and has provided local governments
with the tools and financing to achieve monumental change in a
short period of time.*

## Copenhagen

Copenhagen is the first city in the world to chart public life over the
last five decades so that changes in urban life can be quantified and
studied. The city is routinely selected as one of the most livable in
the world with the highest "happiness" quotient. It is perhaps the
most "bike-friendly" city in the world.

In Copenhagen, bicycles have the priority over cars at most intersections. They use raised sidewalks as one technique to ensure that
bikes can cross streets safely. A staggering 80 percent of residents
have access to bicycles – for kids, it is 96 percent. Copenhagen's
focus on being bike-friendly and its use of the public realm help to
attract families to the city's lively public spaces.

Public transportation is an important part of the city's urban design. The metro subway system is fully automated (i.e., driverless). Regular buses run every two to six minutes.

Copenhagen has no high-rise complexes, either for business or residential. Homes are modest, so the public realm becomes very important; the city encourages great public spaces, such as an artificial waterfront and huge park so people want to come downtown and socialize.

Public art – from the famous "Little Mermaid" to the Tivoli Gardens – attracts visitors from around the world. The city is highly committed to public performances, art, and local cultural activities. It also boasts the Stroget, one of the largest shopping districts in Europe, which has been car-free since the 1960s.

As the Royal Capital of Denmark, with 1.1 million residents, Copenhagen is beautifully planned and designed. Its pledge to sustainability is remarkable, and the residents celebrate and support that every day.

*The Takeaway: Even in a northern climate, Copenhagen's strong commitment to year-round walking and biking, and to public transportation, has resulted in a highly livable city. It offers natural charms, an animated core, and a comfortable family lifestyle. Strong civic leadership has seen this royal capital evolve into a very sustainable city and a world leader in civic environmental responsibility. Its focus on public art, local food, and its heritage and culture have made it a must-see tourist destination, which in turn drives a chunk of the local economy. Copenhagen proves that determined civic leadership can lead the population in a committed and socially accepted lifestyle.*

## Guatemala City, Lima Peru, Mexico City

Grand cities in Central and South America share a number of attributes – Spanish-influenced architecture, bountiful boulevards lined with trees, intricate cathedrals generously adorned with gold. There is a frantic energy on the streets as drivers calculate whether they need a horn or brakes. Public transportation tends to be brightly painted buses, spewing filthy exhaust as they labour up hills and through city streets.

The great heritage and accomplishments of the indigenous people and the astoundingly advanced Mayan, Aztec, and Incan cultures were virtually destroyed centuries ago by their conquerors. Great archeological discoveries of temples, pyramids, and public squares have proven the astonishing design and skills of societies a thousand years ago.

Old-world charms combine throughout South and Central America to offer cities that are historic, yet modern; and bustling, yet with calm, peaceful parks and public spaces. Public art is common. The climate encourages a strong street/sidewalk presence for cafés. Markets teem with foods, crafts, and colourful art.

There is often a certain propensity for danger. Bombs and gunshots are not unknown. Thieves and pickpockets are on the streets. There is grinding poverty and horrible slums; there is great wealth and magnificent homes hidden behind high walls and locked gates. There are sharply divided classes and neighbourhoods.

Pollution is also a problem. Vehicles churn out exhaust fumes at all hours of the day and night. Heavy smog layers often sit over the cities. Potable water is a challenge. Garbage and street cleaning are uncertain.

Yet, despite the challenges of political corruption and a strong military influence, there is an undeniable charm and attraction to these cities. There is warmth from people that is quite extraordinary, and many pockets of calm and beauty in these often chaotic cities. An amazing public garden appears suddenly, or a museum with antique treasures is discovered around the corner.

Every city has its own rhythm; these cities tend to follow the Spanish way of life and business, with mid-day breaks and very late dining. Society is more laid back, and that is reflected in their architecture and urban design. Their government culture is very bureaucratic in nature and operation; it can take a long, frustrating amount of time to get things accomplished in these cities. Building codes are quite different from North America.

Infrastructure renewal and how to pay for it is an immense issue with no apparent solution. Not just in these cities, but in many cities in many countries around the world, we are seeing wonderful heritage properties and important parts of the public infrastructure crumbling. There is a cumulative impact from administrative indifference, local pollution, lack of planned maintenance, abuse by visitors and locals, and inadequate political priorities focused on preserving and protecting these important civic attributes. The end result is endangering the historical culture of cities. These would be terrible losses.

The design of houses is influenced by the local climate, which helps to shape a city and how it functions. Here, sunshine and cool breezes mean an open concept with lovely terraces. Extensive landscaping provides shade and beauty for upscale residences.

Street furniture becomes more important as people enjoy public plazas and socialize together. Spanish culture often dictates where young people may meet, so these spaces are significant. Cities need to pay greater attention to park benches overlooking beaches, and to providing shady corners of parks where kids can giggle and lovers can hold hands.

As millions move into these cities from rural areas, housing and jobs are becoming enormous problems for local governments. Urban transportation is a big, daily problem. The supply of fresh food and water is concerning, as is health care on a full-societal basis. All of these issues are influencing these cities, their plans for renewal and growth, and their security and future.

*The Takeaway: Culture and geography are both strong determinants of how cities are designed, built, and function. Plazas and streets are part of the life and culture of these cities; how the people use these spaces is vital in developing a civil, happy society. Cities in this region have usually been built on revolution. That heritage impacts their structure, both physically and in their society. Investments in infrastructure that have been delayed or ignored are emerging as enormous problems for local governments in cities in many parts of the world, and great heritage buildings and municipal structures are at risk.*

## Las Vegas, Bangkok, New Orleans

Sin cities. There are cities where the dissolute come to play. Cities that make good people do bad things.

Whatever your brand/image/reputation is as a city, it is very hard to change it. It is expensive, takes a lot of time, and may or may not work. The effort by Las Vegas to rebrand itself as a family fun centre, for example, was a dismal failure.

Some cities are overt about their sexuality. Las Vegas proudly shouts its presence in a garish display of neon lights. Hard-partiers wander the Strip, and the chance to get in trouble without trying very hard is prevalent. Their slogan – "What happens in Vegas stays in Vegas" – is a titillating promise of exotic adventures in a comparatively tame environment. The billion dollar casino/hotel complexes offer safe, mainstream stars such as Céline Dion as performers.

A few miles away, brothels are legal. Hookers and escorts advertise openly. Booze is everywhere. Gambling starts from the moment you step off the plane at the airport and never stops. Las Vegas has a façade of glitz and glitter. The city exists to extract from tourists as much money as possible, while giving them a brief and pleasant experience.

New Orleans is more subtle. There is an undercurrent to the city, a laid-back trap for the unwary that some never see until it is too late. Bourbon Street at night (okay, early morning) is a wild party. There are dark, quiet corners and alleys in New Orleans that the temperate and the tentative should never enter.

The Mississippi River flows through the city in a languid manner, and the southern hospitality (waiters will offer you the breakfast wine list at certain restaurants) oozes a special charm. This is a city of mystery, of secrets unspoken, and with a long history of corruption of its government leaders.

Bangkok is a city with many faces. Some of them are very dark, shocking, and unpleasant. Some are open and charming. You can wander through the Golden Palace and then disappear into the night world of sex and drugs from which some never return. The busy hum of tuk-tuks as they speed through city streets and the constant hustle of tourists never stops. The city has grown with little urban planning; streets are a maze, the river bisecting the city is badly polluted, and the architecture is a strange mix of high-rise peaks and sprawling slums.

All cities like these can be dangerous. They can also provide fantastic experiences, great food, fun times, and vacations. This is the dichotomy faced by many cities. What a city wants to be, versus its reputation, are often distant ships passing in the night.

*The Takeaway: Cities have personalities. They can hum, they can be beautiful, they can be cold, they can be exciting, and they can be dangerous. Public places and spaces are critical in shaping a city's personality and image. How a city is operated is crucial. Civic leaders need to better understand the importance of the physical realm and its links to that city's reputation. Local government can influence a city's image through the decisions and investments it makes. Once an image is set in the broad public's mind, however, it is a long, difficult, and expensive process to change that brand/image ... if change can ever be achieved.*

## Auckland, New Zealand

Auckland is a city in transition. Its stated goal is to become the world's most livable city. It has a bold 25-year vision.

As acknowledged by the city's design champion, Ludo Campbell-Reid, "Ten years ago, Auckland needed some healing. [The city] had lost her mojo. With the highest ownership of cars per capita in the world, Auckland was very much built to accommodate the needs of the car, rather than people. Auckland also boasts the highest ownership of boats per capita in the world, and an unrivaled waterfront location, yet people could not easily enjoy a meal while sitting on the harbour's edge. The city had severed itself from the sea."

What is particularly fascinating about this city is the immensity of its vision today, and the commitment to restructure and rebuild the public realm, as well as demand better design and leadership from the private sector.

Auckland's 2012 City Centre Master Plan lays out a dramatic strategy. It identifies six shifts that it considers essential to bring about the transformation that is needed:

1. Dramatically accelerate the prospects of Auckland's children and young people.

2. Strongly commit to environmental action and green growth.

3. Move to outstanding public transport within one network.

4. Radically improve the quality of urban living.

5. Substantially raise the living standards for all Aucklanders and focus on those most in need.

6. Significantly lift Maori social and economic well-being.

The vision is big and so is the price tag – $9B, including the public transit projects and a new harbour crossing. Funding will come from a variety of sources, including the public purse.

The boldness of the thinking and the dollar commitment are what makes this city so interesting to study. "Several developments had gone up which obliterated the view of the water, and [they] just smacked of everything people didn't want. Auckland finally said, we need urban design to be a new focus for the city. Let's be renowned for our design, instead of reviled," says Ludo Campbell-Reid.

"The city has really embraced shared spaces and the new places that have been set up," he adds. Auckland is finding its place in the new world, with the rise of Asia's economic influence and power and the opportunities that are emerging for the nation. "I think New Zealand is a good horse to bet on," he concludes.

As a city of 1.5 million, which is a third of New Zealand's total population, Auckland's development is also very much in the nation's interest. It is going to be a fascinating journey.

*The Takeaway: Transformative projects are by definition big, bold, and visionary. They also come with a big price tag. A city council (and a city) that isn't prepared for the size and scope of exciting and long-term urban design, and the investment and determina-*

*tion it will take to achieve those goals, is usually doomed to failure. Tentative, timid, and small steps are not the answer. Cities need to understand the links between prosperity, strong economies, cultural vibrancy, social expression, environmental responsibilities, strong downtowns, and dramatic urban design for both the public and private realm. Auckland had a courageous look at its situation, understood the need for transformation, and has designed a remarkable vision and plan for the next 25 to 30 years.*

## Songdo and Masdar City

Brand new cities are being built in Asia, the Middle East, Africa, China, and other regions. Western arrogance has sometimes blinded us to the advances of other regions. In fact, Songdo and Masdar City – new, modern cities – may be the wave of the future for bold urban design, funding municipal growth, green technology, and sustainable living.

Songdo, South Korea is built on reclaimed land off the coast near Incheon. It is very technologically advanced and wired beyond belief. 75,000 people live there, 300,000 a day work there. It has become a vibrant business, financial, and commercial hub. The World Bank made Songdo a regional hub. It is within 200 minutes by air of one-third of the world's population.

Songdo is a $40B project. And, importantly, it has been built over the past decade with primarily private sector funding. Yes, private sector.

The city features a Jack Nicklaus-designed golf course, convention centre, performing arts complex, and large central park and water retreat reminiscent of Central Park in New York. Lovely residential and commercial towers spear the sky. It is very green.

Masdar City, Abu Dhabi is in the heart of the oil nations of the United Arab Emirates. The first phase of this brand new city just recently opened. It is designed to be the world's first zero-emission, zero-waste city, powered entirely by renewable energy sources. Welcome to your new competition in the global urban battle. The bar just got raised.

Masdar City is one of the most sustainable communities on earth. It is a model of green urban development. The city's goal is to provide the highest quality of life with the lowest environmental footprint.

As the architect's website explains, "The city itself will be the first modern community in the world to operate without fossil-fuelled vehicles at street level. With a maximum distance of 200 metres to the nearest rapid transport links and amenities, the city is designed to encourage walking, while its shaded streets and courtyards offer an attractive pedestrian environment, sheltered from climatic extremes. The land surrounding the city will contain wind and photovoltaic farms, research fields, and plantations, allowing the community to be entirely energy self-sufficient."

These examples of innovative urban design and thinking are setting new standards for planners and architects. They are stretching the traditional planning concepts and urban design in our city halls. Political leaders need to understand these new opportunities, the innovative design and construction techniques now available, the need for more sustainable development; and they must be prepared to do business with planners, investors, and developers in different ways.

*The Takeaway: Creative, innovative design of new cities and new urban thinking offer great challenges to traditional North American cities, but also great opportunities. Smart cities are realizing that they need to do things differently. Politicians need to up their game to understand the new climate of environmental responsibility for urban centres. Urban planners, designers, growth proponents, and architects are now being challenged about traditional thinking and concepts. We are entering an exciting new era of urban design and development. It will be very different from the past.*

# CHAPTER 11

# A NEW ERA OF INSPIRATION

*"A great city should be an inventory of the possible." – Descartes*

As we lurch into the second half of the second decade of the 21st century, municipalities are facing clear choices about the use of places and spaces, the public realm, planning, urban design, and how to build creative, prosperous, and sustainable communities:

➤ slip back; or

➤ move forward.

To complicate the challenge, many local politicians are confronting the incompatible choice of investing in badly need infrastructure and innovative urban design, or heeding demands from some tax-payers to keep property tax increases around zero.

Under our current structure for governing and financing towns and cities, you can't do both. The system is outdated and needs to change. Municipalities need predictable, secure revenue that is not property tax based. The problem is not limited to North American cities; Melbourne's Lord Mayor Robert Doyle confirmed that trying to get alternative revenue streams is also the biggest problem for Australian cities.

In Canada, sharing of consumption-based taxes is the most apparent solution. Income, sales, gas, and other taxes offer that opportunity; but, most other orders of government want to retain the fiscal hand-cuffs on municipalities. They have little interest in splitting the tax dollar on a fairer basis.

Few municipalities in Canada have the revenue opportunities that most U.S. cities enjoy – and those few in Canada have been very timid in utilizing their expanded powers. It is a huge challenge for elected officials: do they simply hold their hands out and hope for largesse to fall from other orders of government; or, do they have the courage to be held accountable for new taxing authority for their municipalities?

Void of new revenue streams, the choices are bleak for municipal politicians. Provincial and federal governments continue to abdicate their own responsibilities for infrastructure investments and new policies that will remove some shackles from municipalities.

With the vacuum of leadership from other orders of government for encouraging inspired urban design and demanding cutting-edge architecture for public projects, this responsibility falls clearly onto the sloping shoulders of local governments.

"Municipalities need to get together. Don't wait for government to set standards. Enunciate a national policy. Take control of the agenda," urges Jack Diamond.

Absent federal investments and leadership, and lack of focus by provinces and territories on their cities and towns, it is incumbent upon municipalities to push forward. There are encouraging signs that many local government leaders and planners are beginning to support a new era of inspiration, innovation, and stimulation of public places and spaces.

As discussed below, there are a number of critical elements involved in reshaping our cities and building great communities. Fundamental is how municipalities are going to be governed and funded; but, pushing past that is the stark realization that, regardless of those issues, cities today are facing pivotal decisions in their efforts to make them more appealing to job creators and entrepreneurs, and to develop prosperous local economies.

## Transportation

This is a huge issue for every community. Gridlock is getting worse. According to a 2014 Federation of Canadian Municipalities report,

"Across Canada, one-third of municipal roads need significant repairs. Every year, traffic costs the economy $10B in lost productivity, and the average commuter spends 34 days in their car."

Commuters are angry and frustrated. Downtown traffic jams become bigger. Cities are losing the annual pothole battle. Traffic movement slows. "A two-hour daily commute doesn't achieve quality of life," notes Jennifer Keesmaat.

Urban planners know these issues, and now work with traffic engineers to develop solutions. Ideas being implemented include:

➤ better coordination of traffic signals;

➤ greater restrictions on turning/parking/stopping;

➤ stricter enforcement and higher fines for breaking municipal traffic laws;

➤ tolls for some roads and bridges, and for even entering an urban core area;

➤ more high-occupancy vehicle (HOV) lanes to promote less single-occupancy vehicles;

➤ greater support for bike lanes/corridors;

➤ pleasant, safe, and comfortable pedestrian experiences;

➤ better, faster, more reliable public transportation; and

➤ better technology in cars (for example, apps to find alternative routes, etc.).

The big question is whether these are simply sophisticated bandages instead of full-blown solutions. Planners and traffic experts know that the real problem impeding better traffic flow is drivers. That's why self-driving cars and automated vehicles are becoming a reality, with the potential to dramatically change highway travel in the next 25 years.

Traffic congestion can be impacted by encouraging "work where you live" options. That means urban planners and their policies for downtown housing and lifestyles are critical to creating a pleasant, livable atmosphere, making it more appealing to live in higher density areas. Those efforts will take vehicles off the roads – a synergy that will become even more important as the costs for suburban sprawl and exurban living continue to rise.

Many of the most critical urban planning decisions in the next two decades will be driven by transportation issues.

## Housing

The affordability of housing, especially for newcomers trying to enter the market, is a desperate problem in many cities.

"It is my biggest worry," says Larry Beasley. "Not only are we losing the 'creatives,' but we're losing all the craftsmen. [Housing affordability] is the biggest issue. We have just not been able as a society to say alright, let's break through the status quo of how we deliver our housing and start delivering it in a different way. We don't even allow congregate housing (i.e., four or five independent older adults living in one house, sharing a kitchen, each with their own bedroom)."

There are a number of reports that suggest the housing market in some communities in Canada has become overvalued. Young people trying to get into the marketplace are resigned to either buying homes an hour or more from where they work, sharing space with others, or renting forever. The question for a lot of cities is, how do we help them build equity?

"One of our great risks is affordability of housing," says Jennifer Keesmaat. "It is imperative in a city that young people have some way of building equity. That is an important part of having a stable middle class. This is a significant challenge in Toronto right now. There are lots of young, talented people renting condos who can't foresee the day they could buy a condo, or you get those who bought a shoebox condo. It is very difficult for them to imagine living their lives out in that condo or generate the equity in order to upsize for a family."

"I think [cities] need to mandate mix, to ensure there is a certain family component to any project, particularly when people are looking for higher density," observes Jack Diamond.

This is also where the public realm becomes so important. Families need those urban green spaces, safe sidewalks, and public spaces and places to socialize and gather. There is a complex rhythm to street life, and the municipality has a greater role to play.

Cities need to look at different solutions. Co-op housing, social housing, and public housing have all had their moments in the sun. As other orders of government withdrew from housing several years ago, municipalities had to assume a greater role. Now – even as costs rise, the other orders of government continue to fund inadequately, and the availability of rental properties falters – new solutions are emerging.

"As cities become more and more successful, [housing affordability] is going to be a bigger issue," says Larry Beasley. "This is true of cities around the world. They draw demand, there isn't enough supply, and prices go up."

Cities in almost every country are looking for innovation. "Madrid is an interesting example," he says. "They are beginning to think there are more sectors to the housing economy than just the social housing base. They are developing options. Madrid has market-based non-profit home ownership – a sector of housing that is not going up in value, which means over time it gets dramatically more affordable compared to other units. People can own their unit, which means they can build equity."

The affordability of housing (a quite different concept from affordable housing) is emerging as one of the most critical modern challenges for municipalities. Vancouver, Toronto, Fort McMurray, and other cities are facing dramatically higher prices for housing. This impacts Canada's international competitiveness in attracting entrepreneurs and young talent.

Innovation in the housing sector is increasing, with companies now offering "house in a box" designs. A complete house can be shipped in a standard shipping container, and put together easily, for a relatively modest price.

As boomers age, residences for seniors are emerging as a significant concern. Interesting ideas to encourage an active lifestyle for aging residents include onsite pools, game rooms, physical therapy and exercise facilities to keep them active, and social opportunities ranging from onsite libraries to bars, and movie theatres to fine dining.

## Public Places

With the steadily increasing urbanization of society, public places become more significant in daily lives. Municipalities are the clear leaders in providing modern facilities that are so well-used by residents of all ages.

*Libraries* – Although a few will dismiss them as just a warehouse of old books, libraries are cleverly reinventing themselves as one of the most important of all public places. They are free, safe, neutral, and increasingly offer a comfortable social experience complete with cafés and lounge chairs. They appeal to residents of all ages. Free access to computers is still a very important role for libraries.

They also help people seek knowledge. Librarians are, in some ways, the traffic cops on the internet highway, assisting those who need help and protecting the unwary. With books, movies, music, and more now available for download on various handheld units, libraries are mobile and modern. Some libraries provide performing arts space and offer rooms for functions of all types. Some even host social or community agencies.

With the growing awareness by smart communities of the need to improve adult functional literacy and numeracy levels (which directly corresponds to an increase in the local GDP), libraries are the natural repository of community ESL and literacy efforts. And, developing a love of reading by children continues to be one of a library's greatest legacies.

*Community/recreation centres* – These facilities have a greatly expanded role in most neighbourhoods. They are not just a skating rink – they are a fitness centre; provide community meeting spaces; offer important education to encourage public health; provide lifestyle advice to newcomers; and more.

Often, there are interesting green spaces surrounding the complex that may be used for community gardens, outdoor recreation, skateboard parks, walking paths, and many other purposes. These large centres are frequently paired with other civic services – a library, a Y, neighbourhood agencies, and others – to provide a multi-purpose facility.

*Decentralizing city hall* – Efforts are being made to take city services out to the community, rather than driving everything – and everyone – into the downtown city hall. Particularly for social services, this is enabling people to get easier access. In Boston, they dressed up a food truck and have created a mobile city hall that travels out to neighbourhoods.

*Cultural facilities* – Long a feature of most successful and appealing cities, performing arts centres represent a commitment to the arts that many believe is a very important part of building a city that will attract the creative sector, entrepreneurs, and investors. Museums, galleries, and arts hubs are similarly important assets for contemporary, successful cities.

Architects play a crucial role in designing public places. Often, if given the latitude, this is translated into a community expression of art, function, form, and beauty. Municipalities have a rare opportunity to expand their communities' flowering cultural connection to the people when such projects are designed. It is an important civic chance to support a public place that has architectural significance.

## Public Spaces

"There is more public space than just downtown public space," reminds John Nicholson. "Public space helps to define a city. It is shared. There is a risk today of the community being absent."

This key element of encouraging socializing – in an era where human interaction and contact is often diminished – falls to the responsibility of the municipality. Texting and posting selfies on social media sites is not the same as actually having a face-to-face conversation.

"Public space, lakes, river banks, parks ... are natural, but can also be man-made/created. For example, the quadrangles in a university – surrounded by buildings, this public space encourages play, social settings and gathering places, have a coffee, study, but it is all man-made," says John Nicholson.

A municipality is the steward of a considerable amount of public space; parks and natural areas are amongst the most popular of civic amenities. Today's neighbourhoods are usually designed with stormwater management ponds that become attractive community features. Parks, walking paths, and bike/blading paths in and around natural areas are very popular, and can be used for fundraising marathons and events, as well as family picnics and celebrations.

These public spaces are tremendously important for a community. And, increasingly, public spaces in a dense urban setting are a focal point for socialization. People can meet and gather at a specific point in an urban plaza. Like the European piazzas, an attractive urban space is becoming more common in North American cities, and better utilized by people looking for that human contact and interaction, such as lonely seniors

Communities will look at their streets in quite different ways in the future. As they reclaim their streets for the people, exciting new opportunities will emerge to make the street a public space for socializing and shared experiences.

Communities will need to animate these spaces more, and to make them even more appealing. Moveable fountains. Pop-up musical performances. Buskers. Street food trucks. Electronic light shows on buildings. Public art that appears, then goes. Spontaneous happenings. Public spaces are truly becoming our new community living rooms.

## Urban Acupuncture

As dramatic and important as huge transformative plans and projects are to a city's development, there is growing appreciation of the importance of small, precise, local solutions to a particular neighbourhood problem.

These initiatives are usually done on a small scale, but they often help to reshape a community by eliminating a problem or refreshing a property or block. It may involve demolishing an abandoned building, rerouting traffic, giving an incentive to a developer for a particular piece of property, designing a new civic park or green-space, changing how a building interfaces with the street, etc.

Key to success is engaging and involving the local community. Residents must have the opportunity for meaningful input. Often, the initiative will come from the neighbourhood that becomes fed up with crime, pollution, or inaction around a building or street corner. Simple solutions implemented quickly can help to transform that block.

This same urban philosophy can also be adapted for a particular problem in a downtown block or a building. It requires providing remedies that can be swift, effective, and precise.

The public often gets frustrated with municipal planners and others who may appear to hide behind rules and regulations, instead of just solving a neighbourhood problem.

In simple terms, is the municipality going to roll out the red tape, or the red carpet?

## Community Health

There are significant changes in our community health profiles. Diabetes or pre-diabetic conditions/lifestyle now affect nine million Canadians, and is of particular concern in many First Nations communities. Childhood obesity is a problem. So is the aging population.

Planners have a role to play in all of these societal issues. For example, designing safe walking paths to schools; prohibiting fast-food and candy stores in the vicinity of schools; encouraging playing fields and open green spaces near schools; supporting community gardens; including walking and bike paths, as well as skateboard parks in the neighbourhood – all theses things encourage more physical activity for kids.

How neighbourhoods are designed and zoned has an impact. Are there walkable connectors? Are schools integrated with other community facilities? Are trees protected? Is there sufficient green space in neighbourhoods for families to enjoy? Planners need to consider health and lifestyle challenges in their community planning.

Commuting is both stressful and unhealthy. The connections between the suburban car-oriented lifestyle and health concerns are now pretty clear. The quality of air in urban environments is an issue. How we design buildings and roads impacts our environment.

Seniors are becoming a very significant part of every community. They are politically active and often quite firm in what they see as priorities. The physical realities of age, and new hips and knees, mean they often walk a bit slower; so, municipalities are realizing that they have to design intersections and time crossing signals differently. Seniors are bothered by things like ice on sidewalks, so a few communities are starting to think about *heating* their sidewalks – as already happens in Iceland. The savings on "slip and fall" accidents and lawsuits make the idea interesting.

Dementia is a problem that is touching more and more families. There are very significant impacts when a family member begins to suffer from Alzheimer's or dementia. We are not set up to handle the home care issues involved, particularly for aging couples. This will impact future design of social housing and adult care facilities; technology to help locate missing persons; and tools available for municipalities to help seniors age gracefully.

## Gritty Life on the Streets

Homelessness is a problem for every community. Canada has no national strategy. In fact, some municipalities have actually offered homeless people a one-way bus ticket to another community!

Some cities have devised very impressive plans to try to move homeless people into some form of social housing, only to find a lack of support from other orders of government. Municipalities always end up with the responsibility – and cost. They are the government agency of last resort, and they have to look after their citizens.

Police departments will bluntly tell you that they spend millions of dollars taking street people with psychiatric disorders to a hospital, only to see them released because the hospital doesn't have the facilities to look after them. It is an expensive cycle of public money being wasted.

In Honolulu, there are nearly 5,000 people living on their streets. The city has imposed elaborate by-laws restricting use of (i.e., sleeping in) parks and beaches overnight. Patrols are constant. It doesn't seem to have had much impact on the homeless, who become skilled in moving around. But, the city has been smart enough to understand that the problem isn't going away, so they also provide public washrooms, drinking water, public baths and showers, and other amenities to assist those who either choose to or must live on the streets.

Regardless of circumstances, local governments are facing serious challenges in dealing with the growing problem of homelessness.

## Gateways

Towns and cities often underestimate the importance and value of their gateways. Whether it is vehicles arriving from major highways, tourists alighting from the airport or train station, visitors from the harbour, or even the "virtual welcome" on the internet, gateways make a statement about your community.

A little sign huddled in a dusty flower bed on a slope beside a highway exit is hardly a cordial reception. Dirty streets marred by potholes don't send a good message. Neither do junkyards, smoky old manufacturing plants that may well be abandoned, litter beside the road leading out of the airport, and a lack of colourful, easy-to-understand direction signs and community greetings.

Don't look at your gateway through your eyes – look at them with fresh, clear, unblinking reality. Do an exchange with other civic officials – they visit your community, you visit theirs, and then each writes a blunt, honest appraisal of the other's gateways and entrances.

Remember as well that gateways are just as important to welcome people into the downtown or to special districts or precincts, such as an arts district or a historic neighbourhood.

Planners and urban design experts realize that well-designed signs and beautifully landscaped routes offer a lovely statement about their town or city. They impress visitors and also make locals feel great.

## The Buzz

What makes a neighbourhood or community distinct?

"It has a pulse, a hum, or a vibe. You can feel it and identify with it," says Jeff Fielding. "It has to be eccentric – the people are different, even weird. It has to have famous stages – streets, intersections, gathering places, see and be seen. It has to have renown. It has to have celebrity – people of fame need to be present or visit. It has to have gossip – people need to be talking about rumours and events. It has to have setting – waterfront or riverfront. It has to have eclectic architecture – gritty, texture, scale. It has to have great food. It has to have unique entertainment – in particular music. It has to have sex – lust and debauchery. It has to have animation – lights, billboards, graffiti, street people. It has to have discovery – something different than home."

This is the buzz that cities want. That energy, fun, excitement. There are lots of cities in the world, and many of them are bland and boring.

This is why the design elements and flourishes are important. Just as heritage properties can separate one city from another, so can great design. Unique and innovative design makes a special statement about your municipality. Planners, designers, engineers, and architects all need to push the bar. Politicians need to demand more, and then have the courage to support creativity and bold expressions – even when they are controversial or cost a bit more.

That is why the use of colour is so important. As Tessa Virtue reminds us from her experience as a global performer, the vibe from public places and spaces, the atmosphere, the colour, and the feel are both tangible and intangible parts of what make up great experiences in great communities.

Communities often tend toward grey and very safe, neutral colours; warm bright colours instantly change the feel of a street or building. Public art is an important component of public spaces. Planting trees, offering bright flower baskets on street lights, sparkling water features, bright plants, colourful signs, spectacular lighting displays – these all add to the excitement of your community and the pleasure people feel from it.

It is astonishing that some municipalities have easily accommodated food trucks on the streets, while many others have cowered and butchered the issue for years.

Generating buzz through planning and design is a direction that municipal councils, planners, architects, and designers have to make – and they have a choice.

## Living in Urban Settings

How people live in their urban environment is changing. An increasing number of people are choosing to live in a downtown urban setting, usually in a high-rise condo or apartment. Both young people starting out and older folks downsizing are learning how to live comfortably in this realm.

Fewer of them own cars or drive daily. The cost and inconvenience of vehicle ownership is increasingly prohibitive. If they need to drive somewhere, they rent a car by the hour, or for a weekend. That means they carefully plan their trip, stops, and activities.

They walk more. Whether it is several blocks to a subway or bus stop, getting to work, or just walking the dog, they use the sidewalks more. That is also why little green spaces are appealing, and why the street presence and feel are so vital. The street must be safe, animated, lit, and clean.

These urban dwellers shop more often, usually in small boutique shops or specialty stores. Urban drug stores devote half their shelf space to food. As Europeans have known for centuries, daily shopping for food is a healthy way to eat. There are emporiums in underground subway stations, there are small food specialty stores opening in neighbourhoods, and restaurants and delis offer take-out.

They go out more. Sitting in your tiny condo gets boring. So, off they head – eating out, going for a drink, walking in the evening, sitting in parks, visiting the library, or enjoying a free outdoor concert. They are hosting other couples at a restaurant, rather than entertaining at home.

Residents are supportive and protective of their neighbourhood. Paradoxically, living in a very big city often means your own circle of friends and community is quite small. They tend to stay in their immediate neighbourhood, and are observant of change, deterioration, or danger.

They are cosmopolitan. Compact urban living leaves little room for hatred based on gender, race, ethnic background, or religion. There is usually a tolerance for differences and an acceptance of alternative lifestyles and personal decisions. Blended families are more common, and fusion families (those of different cultures) are routine.

Urban residents are usually safe. Bad things can happen anywhere, anytime; but, urban life has generally gotten safer. No one can predict a madman's actions, but urban planners have designed safer streets and improved neighbourhood security through smart planning. Residents learn to be alert, even though life is usually secure.

## Philanthropy: An Investment in a Community

Canada has never embraced philanthropists as great agents of change for municipal government the way the U.S. has. In many American communities, it is a philanthropist who steps forward with large cash in hand to jump-start a particular municipal endeavour or initiative. Often, a foundation or family will gather like-minded individuals and push a municipality into redeveloping an abused area, or will focus on planning bigger, important initiatives to help the community.

These families have often been the foundation of that community. Now, generations later, the kids and grandkids have moved along, the family money has been split many ways, and donations tend to focus on health care or perhaps a particular arts or educational event. Canadian municipalities haven't done a very effective job of seeking and rallying substantial donations/investments from people interested in rebuilding and refurbishing their communities.

The new emphasis is on large funding initiatives to help transform some public policy or design. For example, Dallas drew upon private donations to kick-start a new focus on urban design and improving the city.

"Make a program and policy to do that," says Larry Beasley. "Find small and medium-sized spaces that have been left behind. Identify them and make them better. Private/philanthropy can help develop them. Tap into urban design and landscape expertise in the city. Go out, walk around. The public purse is limited, so we need to involve the private sector. Get people to invest in their community through private sector funding and coordinated giving. Convert the regulatory system from a policing system to a wealth-creating system. Crowdsourcing to fund public art projects. Look for partners, include the public realm in other projects going on. Cities need to retrain, then challenge, staff and politicians to look for new ways of doing business, and find new sources of wealth."

## Connectivity

The issue and opportunity offered by better connectivity has emerged as a significant municipal planning challenge. There is a growing restlessness, an increasing demand by people for better connectivity.

That pressure arises from various factors, starting with the physical connections – taking into consideration how you travel through a community, how neighbourhoods are joined, how traffic patterns impact pedestrian and vehicular movements, and how paths and parks are designed to allow people to interact and communicate. Public transportation has its own set of connectivity concerns – how people get to work, how kids travel to events, and how families travel to see relatives or experience great activities like a Santa Claus parade. Public transportation has to be affordable, safe, reliable, and frequent. In Auckland, the goal is to have every urban resident within a five-minute walk of some form of public transportation.

Another key element is social connectivity – through social media; casual gatherings in public spaces; shared experiences at a food truck; or sitting in a park listening to a concert. Municipalities must be both the enablers and the catalysts as they take on this somewhat new and emerging role for local government.

Without these forms of connectivity, there can be a breakdown of society. There is a danger of people not moving and using the public realm. Locked in a little apartment, sitting on a couch surrounded by media outlets, is not a great way to experience life or contribute to your community.

Connectivity in all of its forms and definitions is growing in significance. It is a clear factor in designing and rebuilding great communities.

## Future of Urban Planning

Jennifer Keesmaat is thoughtful about urban planning in the future. "We really need to become advocates for what we know is sustainable over the long term and for what we know are in the best interests of the public. Part of that is being better informed ourselves, and better understanding decision making and planning outcomes. It's better using data and evidence and analysis in shaping our decision making. We need to build up our own expertise and own credibility and really become a voice for Canadian urbanism."

John Nicholson works with municipal officials on projects every day, and has some pertinent observations about improving the system. "A clear understanding of the rules should be established early. That can be done by meeting with the public at the front end of a project and setting the guidelines. I think there's more to be won by doing developments like that, and it comes back to the idea of having design guidelines at the level of a neighbourhood. If you set the context early, pay attention to timetable, respect history, then I think you're much more likely to get a successful solution. The government needs to set policies – elected officials are there for a reason."

The crucial links between social policy, community wealth generation, and urban design and focus are paramount for Eddie Friel.

"Every single solitary community is now addressing the growth in poverty. Look at the U.S. in the past five years. The level of poverty in upstate New York is an affront to any civilized society ... why do we accept that? We need to get our values rearranged. We've lost the place about people and taking care of people, what our responsibilities as humans are. To have no value system is what we're suffering from at the moment. We can't afford not to care. We have a duty to care. Our duty is to ensure that we rebuild these communities and give them back to people where those who are denied the opportunity of work and the decent quality of life are given that opportunity. But, if our education system is so appalling that we are condemning them to poverty from the age of 10, then we need to ask ourselves some pretty serious questions. It isn't just about having nice pretty places, it is about giving individuals who are denied access the opportunity, the right, to have a decent quality of life."

How municipalities will get there is a long, winding road. That's why this book has been looking at such broad but important issues – we need to start these conversations and find new solutions.

That also means having the courage to examine how cities have always operated. We need to open our minds to the society of tomorrow, because it will be a vastly different world for local government.

Ludo Campbell-Reid knows that how communities view the public realm and public spaces varies around the world, but local urban designers have a unique responsibility. "We are the guardians of that space. We've found that our work has been a catalyst for the private sector. They often haven't seen their responsibilities as outside their boundary. The work we've been doing in our city centre is actually shifting people's perceptions about Auckland."

He also sees governance as a big emerging issue. "Cities around the world have lots of processes in place, but actually governance is going to be one of the biggest issues for the public realm over the next decade."

Larry Beasley also believes governance is crucial to change. "We need to challenge the status quo of regulations. Who controls public space? Street standards? Subdivision standards? Exclusionary zoning standards? Health standards? All those things are putting us in strait jackets. All for good reasons, individually, but the net effect is limiting the urban quality that we can achieve in our country."

Jack Diamond looks ahead to changing that culture. "Excellence is not elitism," he says firmly. "When [our cities or our country have] instances of success, make it a role model. It becomes the gold standard."

He suggests supporting concepts like a Canadian Fund for Innovation for Cities, where municipalities could compete for funds by presenting brilliant ideas. "Maybe we set national targets for cities – density, consumption of water, electricity, set performance standards, then give money to cities that perform best," he says. "That would also allow the private sector to show how to do things better. Innovation. Performance standards."

Melbourne's Lord Mayor Robert Doyle sees several important civic planning initiatives in the future: "You've got to have that continued prosperity of the city, because without that you don't get the activity. You've got to continue to build sustainability – stormwater harvesting, retrofitting buildings, planting of trees, the broadening of footpaths, the taking of cars out of the centre of the city, the increasing of pedestrians and cycling, the built-form of the city – we are custodians of all of that. But, I think the new frontier is resilience. To what extent is your city prepared/capable to cope with seven days of 40 degrees Celsius? To what extent are you going to cope with flooding? Water shortages? To what extent is your city capable of responding to the challenges of the heat island effect, or seasonal changes?"

It is clear from the passionate and thoughtful comments by these leaders that the design, planning, development, and use of our public places and spaces has become one of the most important elements in building great 21st century cities.

While each municipality will look at these concerns and opportunities a bit differently, what is obvious is that they need to better focus on the emerging uses of these places and spaces. Our society is changing, the lifestyle of families is changing, and how we're going to design and pay for great public venues is changing as well.

Throughout the research for this book and my conversations with many civic officials, it became apparent that there is great dissatisfaction with the way things are done today in municipal planning departments.

There is a frustration that planners have become fixated on rules, not solutions. There is a bitter view from the private sector about the public sector, and that isn't useful in finding positive outcomes. We need to push local government to become enablers of great initiatives.

There is also disappointment that government officials don't understand, appreciate, or recognize the importance and beauty of truly innovative design and bold, fresh planning and development concepts. It is a lose-lose situation ... and the biggest loser is the community.

At the same time, however, there are clear signs that thoughtful people are now talking about our public realm and how to make it better. Public places and spaces are now on the civic radar screen like never before. Interesting ideas from municipal planners, people in the community, the private sector, and lots of other areas are coming forward. We also need to give permission for some of these ideas to fail – innovation is not always a clear, straight path forward.

The commitment to improve will take both giant leaps and tiny steps. It is a process.

The design and use of the public realm is a critical part of developing strong local economies. Communities that invest wisely in great public places and spaces, and animate their public realm, are simply better positioned to attract the people who make investments – and create jobs – as well as the innovative minds that fill those good jobs.

Smart communities are leveraging these public assets to improve the quality of life for all residents. That is a pure goal for local government; too often, though, it is not stated clearly and not pursued with passion.

To reach that goal is going to take a dedicated effort to change the culture inside city hall and planning departments. We need a new generation of brave urban designers, and new commitment from the private sector. It will require strong, visionary elected leaders.

It will demand more of local philanthropists and community leaders. They must work together, and with city hall, to set bold targets and timetables for reshaping downtowns, districts, and neighbourhoods. We must share the exhilaration of exciting, creative concepts for building our communities.

The critical links between urban design, great planning concepts, and a prosperous, healthy, sustainable, and vibrant community have never been clearer. There is no more precious responsibility for a municipal council than meeting these vital community goals.

Public places and spaces are becoming our greatest civic legacy.

# MUNICIPAL WORLD
# PUBLICATIONS

To order any of the following Municipal World publications, contact us at mwadmin@municipalworld.com, 519-633-0031 or 1-888-368-6125, or visit <books.municipalworld.com>.

**10 Trends for Smarter Communities** (Hume) – Item 0037

**Brands Buzz & Going Viral** (Chadwick) – Item 0077

**Cultural Planning for Creative Communities** (Hume) – Item 0035

**Deputy Returning Officers Handbook** – Item 1280

**Digital Connections: Social Media for Municipalities & Municipal Politicians** (Chadwick) – Item 0076

**Electing Better Politicians: A Citizen's Guide** (Bens) – Item 0068

**Executive Policy Governance: A Leadership Model for Local Government** (Cuff) – Item 0056

**Guide to Good Municipal Governance** (Tindal) – Item 0080

**Making a Difference: Cuff's Guide for Municipal Leaders Volume 1: A Survival Guide for Elected Officials** (Cuff) – Item 0059-1

**Making a Difference: Cuff's Guide for Municipal Leaders Volume 2: The Case for Effective Governance** (Cuff) – Item 0059-2

**Measuring Up: An Evaluation Toolkit for Local Governments** (Bens) – Item 0061

**Municipal Election Law 2014** – Item 1278

**Municipal Ethics Regimes** (Levine) – Item 0045

**Off the Cuff: A Collection of Writings Volume 1** (Cuff) – Item 0055-1

Off the Cuff: A Collection of Writings Volume 2 (Cuff) – Item 0055-2

Off the Cuff: A Collection of Writings Volume 3 (Cuff) – Item 0055-3

Ontario's Municipal Act – codified consolidation – Item 0010

Ontario's Municipal Conflict of Interest Act: A Handbook (O'Connor/Rust-D'Eye) – Item 0050

Politically Speaking: Media Relations & Communication Strategies for Municipal Politicians (Chadwick) – Item 0075

Procurement: A Practical Guide for Canada's Elected Municipal Leaders (Chamberland) – Item 0070

Public Sector Performance Measurement: Successful Strategies and Tools (Bens) – Item 0060

Rediscovering the Wealth of Places: A Municipal Cultural Planning Handbook for Canadian Communities (Baeker) – Item 0025

Roadmap to Success: Implementing the Strategic Plan (Plant) – Item 0084

Run & Win: A Guide to Succeeding in Municipal Elections Second Edition (Clarke) – Item 0020

Rural Community Economic Development (Caldwell) – Item 0015

Stepping Up to the Climate Change Challenge (Gardner/Noble) – Item 0095

Strategic Planning for Municipalities: A Users' Guide (Plant) – Item 0085

Taking Back Our Cities (Hume) – Item 0034

The Local Food Revolution (Hume) – Item 0036

Town & Gown: From Conflict to Cooperation (Fox) – Item 0065

Truth Picks: Observations on This Thing Called Life (de Jager) – Item 0090

Watch for Gord Hume's new book, *The Leadership Crisis*, coming in 2016.